A YEAR OF COOKING LIKE MUMMYji

A YEAR OF COOKING LIKE MUMMYJI

VICKY BHOGAL

illustrations by Kate Miller

food photographs by Juliet Piddington

poetry extracts by Vicky Bhogal

SIMON & SCHUSTER
A VIACOM COMPANY

In recognition of the indelible print that family leave upon us.
Dedicated with much love and special thanks to Aneil and Karen.

First published in Great Britain by Simon & Schuster UK Ltd, 2006
A Viacom Company

Simon & Schuster UK Ltd
Africa House
64–78 Kingsway
London
WC2B 6AH

1 3 5 7 9 10 8 6 4 2

Designer: Jane Humphrey
Illustrator: Kate Miller
Typesetting: Stylize Digital Artwork Ltd
Poetry extracts: Vicky Bhogal
Photographer: Juliet Piddington
Home ecomonist: Kim Morphew
Food stylist: Helen Trent
Copy-editor: Michèle Clarke
Proofreader: Judith Hannam
Indexer: Helen Peters

Printed and bound in China

ISBN 0 743 25970 X

CONTENTS

Introduction

I now remember with crystal clarity the expression of utter exasperation on my mother's face. I was six years old and the sort of child who was unnervingly neat, inquisitive to the point of being insufferable, unnecessarily voicing an opinion on everything. I would take the rest of the family's tickets – each one with a 12-book capacity – and visit the local library with my Mum during school holidays, returning with piles and piles of assorted books to greedily gobble up and then hungrily go back for more.

Before I cottoned on at junior school that swotty, nerdy kids, who try to read the *Guardian* instead of the *Beano* (I have been reminded of my doing this recently by my *Phupherji*) invariably get shunned by their peers and are picked last in PE, this was who I was at six. I therefore quickly, and regrettably, hid these tendencies from junior school onwards in favour of playing the class clown and not putting my hand up to answer questions I knew the answer to. But there I was, six years old, and this was the little Vicky that my mother had just lost patience with.

'What is this?' she demanded, frowning and flapping a rectangle of white card in the air. It was a letter from the publishers Penguin. A few weeks previously, I had written a collection of poems all about animals (odd in hindsight, given that I have an irrational fear of most creatures, but obviously I thought it would appear cute) – handwritten on sheets of brightly coloured paper – which I then promptly sent off to Penguin for publishing, having found the address for the UK head office at the back of one of my library books. The correspondence that my Mum was clutching said that they were very interested but, given my age, suggested that I find an agent to handle these affairs. My Mum very quickly, and quite rightly, told me to try and behave like a normal Indian child, work hard at school, get good grades to become a doctor or lawyer and leave all such nonsense alone. I didn't have the guts to tell her that a painting I sent in to Tony Hart had been exhibited on *Hartbeat* that week.

I had completely forgotten this memory until reminded of it shortly after the publication of my first book, *Cooking like Mummyji*, in October 2003. I realised that, although when previously asked about whether I had always wanted to be a writer, I had insisted that until April 2002 I had never considered writing or being published, the idea must have been festering there somewhere in my subconscious from this early experience. So the publication of *Cooking like Mummyji* really was a dream come true, and this time around, my Mum couldn't have been happier.

Cooking like Mummyji

As no measurements are used in Indian or British-Asian home cooking, the only real way for British-Asian girls to learn how to cook authentic dishes in the past was to stand in the kitchen at their mother's side, practising for about 20 years and, with luck, they would pick it up. Great idea in the 1970s; not so great in the 21st century. More and more British-Asian mothers now work in full-time jobs, while British-Asian girls have acquired previously unheard of social lives, mobile phones and increasing academic pressures. British-Asian boys too are faced with the problem of not wanting to cook with their mothers at home but have then found themselves lacking a basic knowledge of how to cook their favourite meals while at university.

So I decided to write *Cooking like Mummyji*. A straightforward manual for British-Asians and non-Asians alike with recipes for British-Asian classics and Punjabi favourites, while dispelling a few myths and stereotypes about our food and culture along the way. I wrote it so that the wealth of our recipes is not lost in the trickle of time and, so that nobody's social lives or commitments are compromised, you can just dip in and out of the book as you wish. Therefore, everyone is happy.

Cooking like Mummyji was a book of personal recipes that were British-Asian in general and also specific to my Punjabi Sikh upbringing; it would certainly have been hypocritical of me to talk of anything else with my first venture. However, as there were many British Asians from different religious communities who came up to me having read and enjoyed *Cooking like Mummyji* and said, 'My family is exactly the same' or 'My Mum says just that', but then also eagerly went on to tell me about other dishes that their mothers cooked, I wanted to reflect that in this book. Therefore, you will find dishes here that are from a variety of British-Asian backgrounds.

One particular moment when I felt an enormous sense of pride refers to an account I was told, just after publication, by a young British-Asian girl who had recently started university. She told me that her mother, gripped with desperation, had decided to give her a preparatory crash course in cooking during the summer, and that the experience was a huge disaster. Cue arguing, many appeals to a picture of Guru Nanak Devji by the mother, slamming of doors by the daughter and much crashing of pots and pans. Then the mother saw my book in a store and felt a huge sense of relief as she handed it to her daughter who was living off pasta in her university halls. This girl told me it pretty much salvaged her, by then, fraught relationship with her Mum and she even cooked a dish from it for her mother, to make up properly. I was so pleased with the outcome and, have to say, felt a little Trisha-esque!

Therefore, I must begin this book first and foremost by saying a very big thank you to all those at Simon & Schuster who made the first book possible, the family members who contributed to and inspired it and the media and awarding bodies who have been so thoroughly supportive – but the most deeply felt thank you has to go to those readers who bought the book and expressed their enjoyment of it; I have been very touched by this. I hope you are all now cooking like *mummyji* in your own kitchens!

A Year of Cooking like Mummyji

I hope you all enjoy this second book too, which is very much a follow-up to the first. It captures the essence of the first quarter of a century of my life – especially my childhood – within my family, and all the food that went along with it. It celebrates a certain era. Set against a backdrop of the seasons, which reflect the seasons of life, from birth to maturity, it is a preservation of the experiences and occasions of my youth, of which food was an intrinsic part. For this reason, I have used family album photographs, and also to reassure you that your family was not the only one that had lurid wallpaper and sported dodgy sideburns. And yes, you get to be reacquainted with my family members.

Continuing this theme of celebration, many of the recipes relate to religious festivals and secular occasions throughout the year, ranging from Mother's Day to the summer football season, and including Halloween, Diwali, Indian weddings, Christmas and Chinese New Year. All wonderful excuses to eat as much food as possible.

One of those 'little Vicky' traits that manages to resurface no matter how many attempts I try to suppress it, is that of voicing opinions. There are many social, cultural and political issues that I feel strongly about. One of these is the issue of Fairtrade, of which I am a fervent supporter. I have therefore included two recipes in this book – Cardamom and Gold Chocolate Truffles (page 56) and Fennel Tea (page 167) – that can be made with Fairtrade ingredients and I have included more information about Fairtrade within the recipe introductions. I hope you enjoy them.

However, despite these distinct differences from *Cooking Like Mummyji*, the underlying emphasis is absolutely the same. For those of you who have not come across my first book, the ultimate aim of both is to communicate the following message: The food eaten in the vast majority of Indian restaurants in Britain bears very little resemblance to the food British Asians eat in their homes. This is due to historic, social and economic factors that created a situation in which Indian immigrants found catering to the Western palate necessary for their financial survival here. Indian restaurant food is certainly delicious – I enjoy my chicken tikka masala as much as the next person – but it is as novel to me as to my English friends. Our home food is healthier, simpler, fresher, lighter, does not require a cupboard full of spices for one dish and has a greater breadth of flavour.

Cooking Indian food is not difficult and does not take hours to make. Do you really think that British-Asian mothers spend all day working to come home and spend six hours preparing dinner? We have shortcuts like everyone else, as you will see. And one of the crucial elements I try to get across is that, unlike in baking, it really does not matter if you add a little more or less of, or substitute, some ingredients. The most important thing is to develop a sense of confidence and be more spontaneous and improvisational with your cooking. It is supposed to be fun after all. Customise dishes to your own particular taste, own the recipes in your own unique way. I try to stop people slavishly following recipes – it's not an exam.

Food is inseparable from life; it is a part of our daily routine. Our very existence depends upon it and it is the most basic reason for almost everything else we do in life. We work to put food on the table, to earn our daily bread, to feed our children. Food is intertwined with memory and upbringing, and it is for this reason that both books contain stories about my family. It is impossible for me to distinguish any food memories from those linked to experiences with family or friends.

So come with me on a journey over 25 years of family life, experiences and stuffing my face.

Vicky

All you will need

I recently had a conversation with a rather senior journalist who earnestly, and slightly eagerly, enquired as to where British Asians do their weekly food shopping. 'Are there all these amazing, secret, hidden markets that most of us don't know about, where you go and haggle for vegetables?' she asked. I had to restrain myself from replying, 'Yes, and we still live in mud huts too.' I didn't remind the journalist that we are now in the 21st century but did go on to explain the following: of course we don't shop in secret bazaars – we live next door to you on the same streets and shop in the same leading mainstream supermarkets, eyeing up the same 'buy-one-get-one-free' offers – although, in the case of some of us British Asians, maybe more than most. What most British-Asian families do is take a trip to the Indian shops closest to them once in a while to buy specialist ingredients and also ingredients that they use a lot of on a daily basis, such as *roti* flour, which can be bought in bulk very cheaply. If they live in an area like Southall or Leicester, they will go more often, whereas families who do not live in predominantly Asian areas, such as my parents who live in Norfolk, go once every six months or so. However, this is not essential nowadays as more and more supermarkets stock all the basic ingredients, even stocking Indian brands, and there are also mail-order websites on the Internet. We don't use 30 different spices for one dish and begin each day by grinding them with a big stone, so don't worry.

For some particular recipes, where I point out that shortcuts or substitutes are unsuitable, it is essential that you use the correct utensils or ingredients. So for these I recommend taking a trip to the nearest Indian area. Make it a day out by also visiting the fantastic clothes shops, catching an Indian film at the cinema and stocking up on specialist ingredients that are available very inexpensively and have a long cupboard, or freezer, life. See my guide below for basic and specialist ingredients and utensils, plus core techniques and tips. I give measurements in cups and spoons to train the eye, so that, eventually, you will be able to cook these dishes without measurements. I have also included a guide to metric and imperial weight equivalents for main ingredients (page 21).

Utensils and equipment – basic

Frying pan This is required for a variety of uses, so make sure you get a good quality one, preferably non-stick.

Large saucepans with lids I recommend a large – both wide and deep – stainless steel saucepan with a lid (even better if it has a see-through lid). Non-stick pans with black coating make it very difficult to see the true colour of the spices and onions, and therefore you run the risk of not cooking them for the correct length of time. However, for some dishes, a non-stick pan will be required, so it is best to have one of each variety, both with lids. The reason why I recommend large pans is that often a lot of water is added, or sauces bubble up, or room is required to manoeuvre the ingredients.

Tongs Long, flat, sturdy tongs will prove indispensable, especially for turning over items cooking on grills and barbecues.

Rolling pin This is used to roll out breads, so make sure you get a good quality wooden one.

Chopping board Although most British Asians and Indians chop vegetables in their hands, you must exercise safety at all times. Good quality chopping boards are necessary for cutting meat on too, and separate ones are often used to roll out breads.

Measuring spoons I use a very inexpensive measuring spoon set consisting of a tablespoon, teaspoon, half teaspoon and quarter teaspoon. They are the simplest of measurements until you become confident enough to cook without them.

Mini-blender or grinder This will save you a lot of time and can be used to whizz up canned tomatoes, onions and chillies. You can also get little hand-held ones from Indian shops that cost little more than a couple of pounds.

Sharp knife We use sharp little vegetable knives at home (apart from when cutting meat), as they are handy for cutting foods in your hands or on a board. While filming for television recently, I got handed a knife that was practically a machete and was encouraged to learn the speedy precision style of board chopping favoured by professional chefs. I refused on the basis that it wasn't the way I had been taught to chop by my mother and I was very happy with my own authentic style. Don't worry about such cookery snobbery and cut the way you feel most comfortable, I say. You're cooking for yourself, your family and friends, not for guests in a Michelin-star restaurant.

Colander A must for draining vegetables and meat before adding to the pan. Line with kitchen paper and also use it to drain snacks straight from the deep-fryer.

Wooden spoon Traditionally, women use a *karchhi*, which is a large metal spoon, for mixing but, as these scrape against the pan and become hot, it is better to use a large wooden spoon with a long handle instead.

Wooden spatula This is good for stirring delicate ingredients and mashing up potatoes.

Fish slice This has many uses, including turning over *parathe*, quesadillas and snacks as they deep-fry.

Can opener Well, we wouldn't get very far without one of these now, would we?

Measuring cups These inexpensive and easily available sets comprise of a one cup, half cup, third cup and quarter cup. They are perfect for training the eye to use visual measurements, which will eventually lead to being able to cook without measures at all.

Kitchen paper Used to drain fried snacks and handy to have around in the kitchen, much more hygienic than cloths and towels – but don't forget to put used sheets in the recycling bin!

Baking dishes A basic utensil for any dishes that need to be baked in the oven.

Aluminium foil Use a good quality foil for covering dishes to be cooked in the oven or for keeping food, especially breads, warm.

Deep-fryer Most British-Asian families have a large, deep metal pan, which they fill up with oil to deep-fry. However, an actual deep-fryer – such as a chip-fryer – is much safer, as you can regulate the temperature. Never leave it unattended, not even for a second, making sure that you have all you need to hand in advance. Also, before switching the fryer on, remove the chip-fryer basket when deep-frying Indian food or you will find the batter gets stuck to the wire basket and the food will be ruined.

More specialised items

Thawa This cast-iron flat griddle has a large black flat-plate and a long tapering handle. Seek one out at an Indian store; they cost under £10 and are absolutely vital for making Indian breads such as *parathe* – a large frying pan will never create the results you want. Wash gently with a soapy non-abrasive sponge after using, making sure any burnt bits of bread are gently removed, but do not use a wire wool brush on it. Always preheat it on a low heat before cooking on it.

Large perforated spoon Get one with a long handle with a wooden or plastic section at the top, so that your hands will not burn. This large perforated metal disc with very smal holes is perfect for making sweet *bhoondi* and also for dropping and retrieving snacks in and out of the deep-fryer.

Drinks blender These are necessary for making *lassis* and fruit milks, but shouldn't be too expensive.

Slotted spoon Use this to remove deep-fried snacks from the oil.

Pestle and mortar These are great for smashing up spices such as cardamom pods for tea.

Metal steaming rack This is used for steaming *idlis* and *dhokla* and may be a little tricky to find. Some Indian shops sell specific *idli* and *dhokla* steamers but I found a rack which cost around £1.50 from the kitchenware section of a large department store. They explained that it is usually used in Chinese cooking for making steamed dishes. The way to use it is to place it inside a deep wok (so that it sits on the sides, not touching the water underneath). An egg poacher or tray can be placed on top of the ring and the concave wok lid is placed on top to seal in the steam.

Metal egg poacher Used specifically for cooking *idli*, it is best to find a lightweight metal egg poacher that cooks several at a time. Mine cooks three at a time and cost a little over £2. It is also useful to get one that will balance well on the steaming rack.

These are all the key, and most important, ingredients that are frequently used to make simple *sabjia*, *roti*, rice and meat dishes. Have these to hand at all times and you can rustle up delicious dishes in minutes. Add the specialised ingredients as and when you need them for specific recipes.

Spices and flavourings

Salt Use a good quality fine table salt and only use coarse rock or sea salt from the mill where specified. Salt is also wonderful for sore throats – pour a teaspoonful into half a cup of warm water and gargle with it thoroughly before bed. It soothes the soreness and helps to kill off any infection. My Dad always recommends it at the first sign of any sore throat or cold, and it always works.

Garam masala I consider this to be the one most vital ingredient, and cannot stress it enough. This spice blend (typically of coriander seeds, black peppercorns, cumin seeds, cassia bark, brown cardamom, bay leaves and cloves) is used in almost everything we make, even some desserts, and gives that truly Indian flavour to anything to which it is added. It is easily bought from all supermarkets but do try and buy a good quality Indian brand of dark brown *garam masala* as some Western brands are very yellow from the addition of turmeric powder, which is not traditional and makes it taste more like a weak curry powder than an earthy, smoky full flavoured *garam masala*.

Ground turmeric A member of the ginger family, this bright yellow powder is mostly used to add colour and a touch of flavour. Don't use too much or it will give a bitter taste. It is this that sometimes makes your fingers yellow when eating food and that colours cheap versions of *pilau* rice. Also easily available from supermarkets, try and buy a good quality Indian brand and keep in an airtight container in a cool, dry, dark cupboard.

Fresh ingredients

Fresh coriander This wonderful green leaf is packed with aromatic flavour and is often added both during cooking and also at the end. This is actually very important – it has been drummed into my head since I was about eight years old! The coriander sprinkled on top at the end of cooking is in no way merely a pretty garnish but adds the final element of flavour too. Any Indian home dish served without this would be considered incomplete. Not only would it look shoddy, aesthetically unpleasing and as if you haven't made an effort, it would also taste wrong. By omitting this part you may cause offence to Indian guests and may as well not have bothered cooking the dish at all. We keep a very large bag of frozen chopped coriander in the freezer and the act of grabbing a handful and sprinkling over the top of a cooked dish is almost a reflex and takes seconds. See page 22 on how to prepare and freeze coriander so that you always have it to hand. Alternatively, as supermarket packets of fresh herbs are so clean nowadays, you can even buy a bunch or packet of fresh coriander and, without chopping, put it straight into the freezer; then, when you need some, you just simply break and crumble some away. You can do this with all herbs such as mint or basil too.

Garlic Strong in flavour, this is used alongside onions in the frying stage. See page 23 on how to peel and cut garlic.

Ginger Fresh root ginger is used frequently to give heat and a delicious flavour; it is also very good for you. Boil a piece of fresh ginger in water for a hot ginger tea to ease a cold. It helps to eliminate germs and toxins within your system. See page 22 for how to prepare and freeze ginger for easier use.

Chillies Fresh green chillies are used in most of our home cooking to give that unmistakeable but fresh tasting bite. One point I must make though is that we chop the entire chilli finely and do not de-seed it, as the seeds contain the most heat and flavour. So chop and add seeds and all! Along with forcing out the bacteria of a cold, the *ayurvedic* system also states that chillies can fire the metabolism, raising it by 25–50% for up to 3 hours. However, before you get too excited, chilli can also increase appetite.

Onions Onions are the base ingredient of a *tarka* to create the sauce for most dishes and are therefore needed at all times. Regular white onions are best.

Tomatoes We occasionally use fresh tomatoes but mostly it is the canned variety, with their slightly sour taste, that is the staple of our sauces. Buy whole plum or chopped canned tomatoes and add as indicated; some dishes require them to be whizzed in a blender first. A great tip I have recently picked up from a friend, to eliminate the stage of whizzing, is to buy passata instead. Make sure it is just tomato though, without herbs or any other flavourings. However, canned tomatoes can be bought very inexpensively, so it is worth always keeping a couple of cans in the cupboard.

Potatoes These are used in many recipes, sometimes as a secondary vegetable. They are therefore a good basic food to have in at all times.

Storecupboard and fridge basics

Oil Which oil you use is up to personal preference, but do not use virgin or extra-virgin olive oil as it burns very easily and has a strong flavour, which interferes with the balance of flavours of the other ingredients. Popular choices are sunflower, rapeseed, vegetable or mild olive oil.

Rice Always use a good quality Indian brand basmati rice and never short-grain or any other type.

Roti flour Indian grocers sell very large bags, which could last you a long time. Smaller packets are now available from almost all supermarkets. Choose from white, brown or wholemeal wheat flour as you prefer. My family uses wholemeal.

Yogurt Good for the digestive system and quite a staple, natural, low-fat, set yogurt is eaten nearly every mealtime and goes with everything. It is an indispensable part of the meal, creating a balanced diet, and is essential for counterbalancing the chillies in dishes. We mix it thoroughly with enough milk until smooth, though some families eat it quite runny, while others eat it still in its set form. It is also used in cooking as a souring agent. Choose a supermarket natural yogurt in whichever consistency you prefer.

More specialised ingredients

The following are the specialist ingredients required for the recipes in this book. Some can be found in mainstream supermarkets but all can be found in large Indian shops.

Spices and flavourings

Black pepper Peppercorns in a mill are much better than the ready-ground versions. You can then remove some peppercorns and smash them in the pestle and mortar if a recipe calls for cracked black pepper or simply grind them in the mill for finer pepper.

Cumin seeds Often fried at the beginning of the cooking process, these give a warm flavour and a pungent aroma. They have digestive properties and release flavour upon heating.

Panch puran Packets of these seed mixtures, which originate from the Bay of Bengal region, are available from Indian grocers. *Panch* means 'five' and here are the five spices: fennel, cumin, onion, fenugreek and mustard seeds. When fried, they release a strong and tangy flavour which is unmistakeable and are mostly used as a pickling spice.

Asafoetida Traces of this unusually flavoured, strong spice are used in some dishes, mainly those of South Indian, Gujarati and Bengali origin.

Bay leaves These give a soft, deep flavour to sauces and to baked dishes.

Cardamoms, brown These are larger and have a deeper flavour than their green counterparts. They are woody, earthy and nutmeggy. Smash and add to sauces and tea, but do not eat.

Cardamoms, green Stunning to the eye; these pods are used in many dishes, desserts and also tea and impart a distinctive bittersweet flavour. They have quite a heady bittersweet, slightly perfume-like aroma. Again, do not eat them.

Cassia bark These pieces of bark have a sweetish, incense-like, woody, musky aroma, a bit like trees just after it has rained. They add a distinct flavour to sauces and desserts.

Cinnamon Thinner and smoother than cassia bark, it has a slightly more savoury taste. Boil a smashed up stick of cinnamon in a pan with water to create an infusion you can gargle with to combat bad breath.

Cloves Used whole in many sauces and desserts, these give a strong flavour and scent.

Coriander seeds Warm and fragrant, these have a mild woody taste.

Dried mango powder Unripe green mangoes are peeled and dried in the Indian sunshine and then finely ground to add a tangy fruitiness to sauces and snacks.

Dried red chilli flakes These are very fiery and give plenty of zest and flavour to snacks and sauces.

Fennel seeds Hugely aromatic and with digestive properties, these seeds are often used for pickling and in making tea. Fennel seeds steeped in boiling water to create an infusion are also used to relieve constipation and can also help to break down the fat in your body and so aids weight loss.

Fenugreek, dried Sold in packets, this is quite dissimilar to fresh *methi* and is added in its dried form to snacks. Some packets recommend using in the place of fresh *methi* by soaking in water, but I prefer to use fresh leaves.

Mustard seeds, black These tiny black seeds are heated to give off their particular flavour.

Pomegranate seed powder Made from crushed pomegranate seeds, this powder gives a fantastic sweet and sour taste and is perfect for fillings and fried snacks.

Saffron Famously the most expensive spice in the world, saffron is used sparingly to add a golden colour and a delicate sweet flavour.

Tukmaria seeds Also known as *sabja* seeds or *grains basilic*. They are tiny black seeds, supposed to have a cooling effect on the stomach. They swell up when soaked and are very commonly used in *falooda*.

Tandoori masala powder This dark red powder is made from coriander, red chilli, cumin, black pepper, ginger, cardamom, bay leaves, fenugreek, garlic, cloves, salt and a little oil. It gives a deep, rich spiciness and slightly sour taste when added in a very small quantity to sauces. Used in a marinade, it gives that delicious flavour which makes *tandoori* chicken such a delight.

Curry leaves These aromatic, peppery leaves have nothing to do with 'curry' and therefore taste nothing like a *tikka masala*. Instead, these brittle, dried green leaves of the neem tree are used to add a pungent flavour to South Indian dishes.

Nigella seeds (kalonji) You will recognise these tiny black seeds as the ones sprinkled over *naan* bread. They are also known as *kala jeera*, small fennel and black cumin.

Ground cumin Ground cumin seeds are an ingredient often used with meat dishes or to flavour street-style snack foods and sauces.

Ground coriander This mild, fragrant powder is often used in conjunction with ground cumin and also gives a musky depth to meat dishes.

Storecupboard ingredients

Food colourings Use these pretty powders or liquids to colour batters for deep-fried snacks or milk-based sweets.

Gram flour (besan) This flour is made from ground pulses very similar to chickpeas. It is widely used for making batters for snacks and breads, and is a fantastic alternative for those who are wheat intolerant.

Rice flour/ground rice Used for making sweets, pancakes and dumplings. Mix with a few drops of almond oil and warm water to make a face scrub.

Rose water This delicate fragrant water is added to desserts and drinks for an angelic touch.

Desiccated coconut Used for sweets and chutneys – comes in fine and medium. Fine is usually used for desserts.

Rose syrup This thick, pink, intensely sweet syrup adds a powerful flavour.

Coarse semolina With its slightly gritty texture, this is delicious when turned into sweet desserts.

Sevian Thin vermicelli noodles are available at supermarkets to make desserts with.

China grass Also known as agar-agar, these fine noodle strands are a type of gelatine extracted from seaweed. They are used in Indian desserts such as *falooda*.

Jaggery (gur) This unrefined brown sugar made from sugar cane juice comes in solid blocks and has an earthy, toffee-like sweetness when melted.

Honey A delicious alternative to refined sugar, try to use an organic variety wherever possible. Due to its soothing, antiseptic and moisturising properties, it is commonly used with lemon as a cough mixture. However, it is also nothing short of miraculous for the skin. Try my honey facial for smooth, clear, glowing skin:

1 Tie your hair back tightly.

2 Smear clear, runny honey over your clean, but dry, face as you would a face mask. It will feel very odd and sticky, but trust me.

3 Fill a sink (or bowl) with hot water and steam your face over it, underneath a towel, for a few minutes.

4 When the steam has begun to dissolve the honey on your face, remove the towel and gently massage it into your skin.

5 Dip a clean flannel into the hot water in the sink, wring out, wipe your face and then press it onto the skin to steam again. Repeat this process with the flannel several times, dipping, wringing, wiping and pressing. There should be no honey left on your face and it should feel smooth and look radiant.

According to the *ayurvedic* system, honey also has weight-reducing properties.

Sultanas, green Green sultanas can be bought from Indian grocers and are smaller, firmer, greener and not as sweet as the golden variety. If you can't get hold of them, golden sultanas or raisins are fine to use instead.

Tamarind You can buy blocks of this compressed sour fruit, to which boiling water is added, to make a tamarind water to add to sauces or make into a chutney. Be sure to remove the stones when it has dissolved.

Pulses

Chana dhal (split chickpeas) This is a very common Indian *dhal*. These split yellow peas are small and sweetish in flavour.

Moong dhal (whole mung beans) These shiny green oval beans are very nutritious and are easy to digest.

Thomi mahaar dhal (urid dhal) These are split *urid* beans with their skins removed, leaving a creamy textured, white *dhal* that has a mild, nutty flavour and texture.

Fridge ingredients

Butter Use a good-quality butter where referred to and never, ever, margarine.

Paneer This milky, firm, very mild Indian cream cheese comes in blocks and is now starting to appear on supermarket shelves. Eat cooked, never raw.

Fresh vegetables, fruit and nuts

Almonds Flaked, chopped or ground, these milky nuts give a creamy sweetness to desserts, rice and sauces.

Fenugreek, fresh This richly flavoured leaf is often added to vegetables and breads. See page 22 on how to prepare and freeze fenugreek.

Lemons or limes Used frequently to sour sauces, keep fresh lemons and limes in the fridge and also a bottle of lemon juice in the cupboard.

Mint leaves Use these fantastically fresh flavoured leaves for drinks, chutneys and breads. Boil mint leaves in water for a mint tea to relieve stomach upsets and digestive disorders, especially bloating.

Pistachio nuts These green nuts add flavour and colour.

Red chillies, fresh Much stronger than green chillies, these are rarely used in cooking but are great in very small quantities and look fantastic for presentation.

Drumstick Long, thin pod vegetable with soft inner seeds, from South India.

Measuring ingredients

Indians and British Asians rarely use scales; traditionally, ingredients are measured by eye but it takes a long time to learn to do this. One of the simplest ways to measure ingredients (until you're able to visualise quantities) is in spoons or cup measures, depending on the amount, and this is the way ingredients have been specified in the book as far as possible.

A standard measuring cup holds 250 ml (8 fl oz). This means that three-quarters of a cup is 175 ml (6 fl oz), half a cup is 125 ml (4 fl oz) and quarter of a cup is 50 ml (2 fl oz). Solid ingredients as well as liquid ones can be measured in spoons or cups.

Measuring common ingredients by cup

1 cup *roti* or *gram* flour . . . . 125 g (4½ oz)

1 cup uncooked basmati rice . . . . 225 g (8 oz)

1 cup granulated sugar . . . . 250 g (9 oz)

1 cup *chana dhal* (split chickpeas) . . . . 200 g (7 oz)

1 cup *moong dhal* (whole mung beans) . . . . 200 g (7 oz)

1 cup *thomi mahaar dhal* (washed, split *urid* beans or *urid dhal*). . . . . 200 g (7 oz)

1 cup coarse semolina . . . . 200 g (7 oz)

1 cup natural yogurt . . . . 250 g (9 oz)

1 cup butter . . . . 250 g (9 oz)

1 cup frozen peas . . . . 125 g (4½ oz)

1 cup canned chopped tomatoes . . . . 225 g (8 oz)

1 cup halved cashews . . . . 125 g (4½ oz)

1 cup chopped pistachios . . . . 125 g (4½ oz)

1 cup shelled mixed nuts . . . . 125 g (4½ oz)

1 cup peeled cooked prawns . . . . 150 g (5½ oz)

Shopping and stocking up

Buying spices Only buy good quality Indian brands from a supermarket or Indian shop. Brands such as Rajah, Natco and East End are always good bets.

Freezing ginger Ginger is used a lot and is a main ingredient in almost every *tarka*. Therefore you need it close to hand and it is helpful not to have to keep buying it fresh and prepare it from scratch every time. Buy 450 g (1 lb) of fresh root ginger. Peel and then grate it all into a large bowl. Shape into teaspoon-sized balls and freeze in a large bag. Whenever you need ginger for a *tarka*, you simply reach into the freezer and drop a ball or two straight into the pan.

Freezing coriander Coriander is also always needed and defrosts easily on contact. Families buy about four large bunches and wash thoroughly. Holding tightly, use a sharp knife to chop finely (including the stalks). Place into large bags and freeze. Break off a handful straight from the freezer whenever needed and sprinkle straight into sauces or on to food.

Freezing chillies Always remember to wash your hands after handling chilli or you will be screaming at the top of your lungs when you touch your eyes with chilli fingers. Buy 450 g (1 lb) of green chillies and remove the stalks. Grind one finely in a mini grinder or chop finely with a sharp knife, seeds and all, and see how much one constitutes (it should be a few flakes). That is your guide. Grind the rest of the chillies and freeze in ice-cube trays. Turn out the cubes when frozen, place in a large bag and keep in a freezer. One whole ice cube of chilli is about eight to nine whole chillies. Slice off the required amount when needed with a sharp knife. Alternatively, take the stalks off and freeze whole green chillies. Simply remove one from the freezer when needed, let it thaw a little and then chop or grind and put straight into the pan.

Freezing fenugreek Buy the desired quantity – one bunch if used rarely and about four if used frequently. Wash thoroughly. Remove the leaves and discard the stalks. Chop finely with a knife, place in a bag and freeze.

Preparation

Size of vegetables, fruit, eggs, etc. This is always medium-size, unless specifically stated as otherwise in the ingredients list.

Washing ingredients One of the things my mother instilled in me was to always wash meat before cooking, to clean it thoroughly and remove excess fat, even if it is packed as ready to go (such as skinned and diced chicken). Years ago, I made some meat on the bone without washing and it was noticed as little bits of blood and skin remained. Quite unpleasant. We usually wash cut meat, fish or vegetables before doing anything else and leave them draining in colanders until it is time to add them to the sauce.

Removing the smell of onion and garlic from fingers One of the most common complaints about cooking Indian food is that all the chopping of onions and garlic can leave you with less than fragrant fingers. However, this very simple tip should help alleviate this antisocial aspect. Simply wash your hands and then run your damp fingers over some stainless steel. If you have a stainless steel tap then just rub this with your fingers and the smell should disappear!

Cutting vegetables in your hands

Indians and British Asians don't usually use chopping boards for vegetables, although they use them for meat, of course. Cutting vegetables in my hands was one of the techniques I had to learn quite young. It means that, often, you can be cutting one thing while keeping an eye on another. Usually, the item is held in the palm of the left hand and carefully cut with a sharp knife in the right. Although I would get funny looks if I started using chopping boards, you should maintain safety at all times.

Cutting onion Usually, it is topped and tailed and the skin is peeled off. It is then cut in half lengthways. Using a sharp knife, cut (but not right through to the other side) at small intervals down lengthways and then down widthways (creating a criss-cross). You then take the knife and slice right across the onion at small intervals widthways. Tiny squares should fall away.

Peeling and cutting garlic Garlic peel is very sticky so the best way is to take the flat edge of a large knife and press on to the clove of garlic until you hear a crunch. The skin should now just peel away in one go. Take the clove of garlic, and very carefully, cut at small intervals down widthways and then once down the middle lengthways (but not right through) creating a criss-cross. Then cut across very finely so that tiny squares fall away.

Cooking

Cooking a tarka This refers to the stage consisting of frying the onion in oil with a variety of other ingredients (depending upon the recipe), such as garlic, ginger, chillies, *garam masala*, salt, coriander, turmeric powder and other spices. It creates the base for the sauce and is the most essential part of the cooking process. If this part is not done correctly, the whole dish will be ruined.

The basic tarka method

1 Heat the oil (do not add ingredients to cold oil in a pan, as this will give an unpleasant flavour and too much oil will be soaked up). If you are frying cumin, only fry for a few seconds until it is sizzling – cumin burns easily so keep a close eye on it.

2 Add the chopped onion and garlic. Almost always use finely chopped garlic as opposed to crushed as this gives a more rounded flavour – crushed garlic is too strong and bitter. If the onions are to be blended in a mini-blender, then keep them soft and white; otherwise, fry until golden brown for vegetables and deep golden brown for meat dishes (check the individual recipes). If the onions are not cooked properly, the whole dish will have a weak taste. But do not burn! Unless the onions are to be blended, make sure they are finely chopped otherwise they will not melt into the sauce and you will have pieces of onion floating around.

3 When the onions are golden, reduce the heat and wait for a minute, or remove pan from the heat. This is to stop everything making a splatter when you add the tomatoes.

4 Stir the tomatoes in and return to the hob, keeping the heat low.

5 Quickly add the other ingredients – ginger, chilli, coriander leaves, salt, turmeric and *garam masala* – and stir well.

6 Now this is the vital part of the *tarka* stage. It is referred to as *raara*. Keep on a low heat and cook for about 5–10 minutes until the mixture has become very shiny and the oil has separated. Keep stirring throughout, adding splashes of water if it becomes too dry.

7 Press the onions into the tomato mixture to get an even sauce. Only when the mixture is shiny with the oil clearly separated do you add the next ingredients. This stage is so important: the onions are blending into the sauce, the spices are cooking and releasing their flavour, the tomato is getting fully cooked, the ginger is melting down and all the flavours are binding together. If you are hasty with this stage you may as well forget the whole thing. The secret to fantastic Indian food lies in getting this right. Patience is a virtue remember!

Cooking roti I don't know a single Indian person who uses the word 'chapatti'. Most people call this bread *roti* at home. I suppose the technical term for this particular recipe is *phulke* as the method includes the stage where the *roti* is puffed up on the open flame. (Traditionally, *phulke* refers to large, thin *roti* made in *gurudwaras* for Langar in India, which are always puffed up on a naked flame.) Some people don't do this stage and simply pat with a tea towel but that is not the way my family and I make them. Of all the items an Indian girl learns how to make, these are the hardest to master. Getting them perfectly round, all the same size, with just enough brown spots, puffed up and evenly cooked, and yet still soft takes years of practice.

Until recently, girls were still expected to use their bare hands in the flames to turn them over but now people are cottoning on a little to fire hazard issues. Therefore, although the use of *chimta* (tongs) is sometimes frowned upon as being a wimpy cop-out, it is slowly being accepted. In any case, this can only be done if you have a gas hob; otherwise, lightly press each side of the *roti* on the *thawa* with a clean tea towel to puff them up gently. When you see light brown spots, the *roti* is cooked. *Rotia* are best eaten immediately but they can be wrapped in foil to keep warm for a short while.

These took me years to learn how to make and I discovered that the secret is all in the timing. Therefore I have tried to be as precise as possible with this recipe. Have fun practising!
Makes 6

2 cups roti flour, white, brown or wholemeal

a little butter

The basic roti method

1 Place the flour in a large, shallow mixing bowl. Using your hands, add water very slowly to bind the flour together. Wash your hands.

2 Knead the dough thoroughly using your knuckles, folding the dough in and turning over repeatedly. Cover and refrigerate for 30 minutes minimum.

3 Rinse the *thawa* and place on a low heat. Take a large shallow dish, fill with *roti* flour and place on the worktop. Get a rolling pin, a plate, a pair of tongs, some butter and a teaspoon.

4 Take the dough and divide into equal portions. Each portion should be the size of a small satsuma.

5 Dust the worktop lightly with some of the flour from the dish. Take a portion of the dough and roll into an even ball in your hands. Place the ball on the work surface and flatten with your fingers. Cup your hands and use the edges of your hands (your little finger side) to make the disc perfectly round. Flatten again with your fingers.

6 Take a rolling pin and gently roll out to form a flat round. Turn over and roll the other side.

7 Lay in the dish of flour to coat, turn over and do the same with the other side. Shake off

excess flour and lay the *roti* on the worktop again. Roll out, using a circular motion to increase the size of the *roti*, and then turn over and roll the other side. Continue this process until you have an even and round *roti* the size of a tea plate. It should not be too thin.

8 Gently pick up the *roti* and gently toss from palm to palm in a pat-a-cake action, rotating the *roti* to shake off excess flour and even out the size. Slap flat on to the centre of the *thawa*. After 4 seconds, when you see the *roti* becoming slightly brown, turn over with the tongs. When small bubbles begin to appear, about 6 seconds, pick up the *roti* with the tongs with one hand whilst moving the *thawa* away from the heat with the other.

9 Place the *roti*, same-side down, straight on to the gas ring, moving it around slightly with the tongs. The *roti* should completely puff up. Turn over immediately for 2 seconds and then return the *thawa* to the ring.

10 Place the *roti*, most-cooked-side upwards, on a plate and spread with a little butter using a teaspoon.

Tips for success

Adding water to sauces Always add boiling water to dishes that are being cooked. This is because the mixture is already hot and adding cold water will reduce the temperature. It will also take longer to cook.

Cooling down sauces with too much chilli We eat yogurt with our meals to counter-balance chilli. If you have put too much chilli in your dish, add a little cream or a touch of sugar to sooth it down. Add these ingredients in minute quantities, tasting as you go. Do not drink water if you have eaten a mouthful of food burning with chilli – water will simply disperse it and make it worse. Have a spoonful of sugar (Mary Poppins style) or yogurt to cool down.

Getting rid of excess salt Take a potato or two, peel and cut into small chunks. Add these to the dish you are cooking with a little water and bring to the boil. Simmer for 20 minutes and then take out the potato and discard. The potato should soak up the excess salt.

Thickening a sauce If your sauce is too watery, take off the lid and boil on a high heat, stirring occasionally to check thickness.

Thinning a sauce If your sauce is too thick, add boiling water, stir and simmer gently.

If a sauce sticks If you find that your meat or vegetables are sticking to the bottom of the pan, do not scrape off the stuck-on residue. Simply add a splash of water, turn the heat very low and cover. The steam will lift it all away.

Ventilation Always remember to have the extractor fan on and the windows open when cooking Indian food to get rid of excess smells. You don't want the smell of frying onions wafting around or sticking to your sofa.

Making dough Add water very slowly in small amounts. When kneading, make sure to knead hard with your right fist (or left if you are left-handed), pressing in with the flat of your knuckles. Then fold the mixture and knead again. Repeat until firm. A good *roti* dough should keep in the fridge for 5 days. If it goes slimy and dark before then, discard. It means that you made too soft a dough. Use less water next time and knead for longer.

What to do if a paratha has gone hard If your *paratha* goes rock hard, it is due to one of two reasons: either you used too little dough (use a larger ball next time) or the *thawa* was on too high a heat. It must be on a very low heat.

Wrapping all breads Keep breads warm and moist by wrapping in foil or a clean tea towel as soon as you cook each one until ready to be eaten.

Cooking rice Always wash rice before cooking: put it in a saucepan and rinse it until the cold water runs clear, as this eliminates the starchiness that causes the stickiness. Treat cooked rice gently. Never, ever, stir or plunge a spoon straight into cooked rice to take a portion. Before serving, always take a fork and lightly graze the surface of the rice to loosen the grains. Work your way through the pan, shaking off any rice that sticks to the fork, so that you have singular grains. Only then should you very gently use a spoon or spatula to take a portion and place on a plate.

Basic ayurvedic principles regarding food

Western medicine is becoming increasingly receptive to and respectful of Eastern holistic medical knowledge. Although certainly not adhered to strictly in any way, and probably out of habit more than anything else, most British-Asian families, mine included, eat meals made up of certain components, all with the aim of providing a balanced diet. For example, we would eat a meat dish (although this is obviously omitted for vegetarians who derive their protein element from the *dhal*), a vegetable dish, sometimes a *dhal*, rice or *roti* of some sort, *dahi* (low-fat yogurt), salad and *achaar* (pickle). These meals are usually very low in fat, made from fresh ingredients and offer a perfect balance of protein, carbohydrates and good fats. The thinking behind this form of meal construction relates to *ayurvedic* principles.

Auyerveda, the Indian holistic science, views the human body, mind and spirit within the framework of a cosmic cyclical journey. It is believed that all material matter, such as plants for example, are made up of the elements fire, water, air, earth and space in various combinations and differing quantities. In relation to humans, it is believed such combinations equate to three constitutions: *vata*, *pitta* and *kapha*, which need to be kept in balance in order to achieve good mental, physical and spiritual health. Diet is instrumental in achieving this and takes into account the personality and physical disposition of the person in question and also the seasons of the year. The point is to provide nutrition through food in accordance with one's own digestive capacities.

To illustrate this, those who are *pitta* benefit from bitter, sweet, astringent and hot food; those who are *vata*, such as myself, are calmed by salty, oily, sour, hot and sweet foods; while it is best for *kapha* to stick to bitter, strong, dry and astringent foods. However, before I rushed out from my diagnosis to happily buy Pringles, dips, chips, cakes, ice-cream and chocolate, someone sat me down and educated me about the various categories.

For example, sweet foods include milk, pulses, cereals and nuts. Sour foods include pomegranate, mango, tamarind and citrus fruits. So, more along the lines of porridge and fruit than Ben & Jerry's.

Foods are also classified in terms of 'hot' and 'cold' foods. By this, I do not refer to physical temperature but physiological impact. 'Cold' foods include green, leafy vegetables, juices, honey, dairy and pulses. 'Hot' foods include grains, eggs, seafood, meat, certain fruits, nuts and spices. According to this *ayurvedic* guide, 'hot' foods, for example, such as meat and fatty sweets, are best eaten in winter. This makes perfect sense when you consider the hearty, insulating foods preferred during cold weather.

Clouds as light as buttermilk pancakes,

The eggshell-blue sky scented with freesia and rosemary,

Daffodils like handfuls of saffron, scattered across the fields,

The birth of the first fruit of the pregnant land,

Cardamom lacing the air...

SPRING

Chicken with baby button mushrooms

Spring is a time for gentle, simple flavours, young and tender meat and sweet baby vegetables fresh from the earth. Here, small, boneless pieces of chicken are smothered in a softly spiced, aromatic sauce – or *thari* as we call it – with juicy whole mushrooms and a crunchy scattering of pale green spring onions. If you think all Indian meat dishes have oily sauces with heavy spices, then your taste buds are in for a fresh surprise. This very healthy, light dish is perfect after the heaviness of winter comfort food, accompanied by simple boiled basmati rice or *roti* with a touch of creamy *dahi* on the side. It is best enjoyed on a mild spring evening after an industrious dose of spring cleaning, which, if it's carried out in anything like the way it is in our house, will certainly leave you hungry! *Serves 4*

Method

2 tablespoons oil

2 teaspoons cumin seeds

1 large onion, finely chopped

1 clove garlic, finely chopped

1 cup canned chopped tomatoes, whizzed in a blender

2 teaspoons grated fresh ginger

2 green chillies, finely chopped

1½ teaspoons salt

1 teaspoon ground turmeric

2 teaspoons garam masala

2 handfuls of chopped coriander

400 g (14 oz) diced boneless chicken

1 packet baby button mushrooms, washed

2 spring onions, very finely chopped

1 Heat the oil in a large pan with the cumin seeds. When they begin to sizzle, add the onion and garlic and fry until golden brown.

2 Remove the pan from the heat for a few seconds and add the tomatoes, ginger, chillies, salt, turmeric, *garam masala* and coriander. Cook on a low heat until the mixture becomes shiny and the oil separates out.

3 Add the chicken and stir-fry for a few minutes, coating well.

4 Add the whole mushrooms, coating with the mixture.

5 Add enough water to just cover the chicken and mushrooms and bring to the boil. Cover and simmer for 20 minutes.

6 Remove the lid, turn up the heat and thicken the sauce slightly for a couple of minutes. Garnish with the spring onion.

Spiced chicken *quesadillas*

I first came across these on a visit to New York in 2003. I am a huge fan of Mexican food and constantly whinge to anyone who'll listen about the lack of Mexican restaurants in Britain. In fact, the prospect of being able to eat as much Mexican food as I could possibly consume was 90% of the reason why I made the trip. Closely followed by burritos, taco salads and enchiladas, which were all available in abundance, it was the delicious quesadilla (from the enormously impressive lunchtime foods chain PAX opposite Macy's, which puts all of our British lunchtime options to shame) that was my clear favourite and led to many a 'tummy on legs' photograph.

Quesadillas are similar to our own Punjabi stuffed *parathe* in that they comprise of thin, crispy layers of bread, in this case flour tortilla, sandwiching succulent hot fillings. You can fill a quesadilla with whatever you like, but some form of cheese (queso) is essential to glue the two tortillas together so that the quesadilla doesn't collapse when you attempt to turn it over. Try this *tandoori*-flavoured Indian chicken variation with oven-roasted peppers, red onion, coriander and melted Cheddar for a light, alfresco spring lunch, accompanied by a green salad and a lemon or yogurt-based dressing. *Serves 2*

Method

1 Preheat the oven to 200°C, Gas Mark 6.

2 Place the pepper strips on a baking tray and drizzle with a little oil. Bake for 10 minutes until slightly charred.

3 Heat the oil in a pan and fry the chicken until lightly golden. Add the *tandoori masala* and salt and continue to fry for 1 minute. Add a squeeze of lime juice and remove from the heat.

4 Heat a large non-stick frying pan and place one of the tortillas on it. Sprinkle on a layer of Cheddar, then some of the chicken, onion, coriander, peppers and another layer of Cheddar. Place another tortilla on top and press down with the flat of your hand to seal it together with the melting cheese.

5 When sealed, use a fish slice to gently flip over the quesadilla and press down on the other side with your hand. Be careful that it doesn't fall apart.

6 When nicely golden and crisp on both sides, use a fish slice to transfer to a plate. Cut into quarters and serve.

½ pepper, cut into long, thin strips

1 teaspoon oil

140 g (5 oz) chopped cooked chicken breast

1 teaspoon tandoori masala

salt, to season

squeeze of lime juice

4 flour tortillas

180 g (6¼ oz) grated Cheddar

¼ red onion thinly sliced

handful of chopped coriander

South Indian vegetables and lentils
in a sweet and hot sauce – Sambhar

The majority of Hindus, and some Sikhs, are completely vegetarian, being opposed to the practice of slaughter for religious sacrifice or consumption. Some Mughal emperors of India also abstained from meat for certain periods of time having become partially assimilated. However, even the majority of those Hindus or Sikhs who do eat meat mostly refrain from eating beef.

The cow is sacred in India (in some parts it is believed to be an incarnation of Laksmhi, the goddess of wealth and prosperity), but is also intensely respected for practical and economic reasons. The cow, or buffalo, is revered as the animal that many Indians depended on in the past, and still do, in a wide variety of ways. As often portrayed in classic Indian movies, one key role is related to their owner's agricultural activities of ploughing and sowing the fields in spring, and also literally carrying their load throughout such activities and while travelling.

This animal provided the family with nourishing milk and even their dung was used. In fact, one of my Mother's earliest memories (and bear in mind she left India for England at the age of five) was to assist in the practice of scooping up handfuls of cow dung, shaping them into patties and then slapping them against mud walls to bake and dry in the sun. These would then be lit and used for fuel for cooking. Her reply to my nose-crinkled expression of distaste at this anecdote was that it was regarded as completely normal practice, and actually rather fun. Therefore, this bovine animal was so essential for their survival, how could they entertain killing and eating it?

This led to Indians, especially Hindus, becoming expert, imaginative and adventurous in cooking vegetarian food. Indian vegetarian food is now widely recognised as being the best vegetarian food in the world, with a huge variety of ingredients and flavours used. This cuisine is a far cry from the western one-flavour-fits-all style of vegetarian food, that leaves you hungrier than you were before, often comprising purely of beans, celery and insipid tomato sauce. Indian vegetarian food embraces such a wide breadth of flavours and textures and is so hearty that many carnivores often fail to notice the absence of meat from their meal at all.

This popular, tangy, hot and sweet South Indian dish, flavoured with jaggery and tamarind, has the consistency of a thin vegetable soup. It is made with split chickpeas, aubergine and tomato, tempered with mustard seeds, *asafoetida* and curry leaves. It also uses an unusual vegetable called drumstick, which is a very long, thin, green, ridged, pod-like vegetable with tender inner seeds. Omit this ingredient if you cannot find it, as there isn't really any form of substitute.

Sambhar is typically served as an accompaniment, along with coconut chutney, to *idli* for a light, highly flavoursome weekend breakfast or brunch, or eaten on its own as a nourishing and warming broth. *Serves 6–8*

Method

1 Place the *dhal* in a pan with 3 cups of water, the turmeric, green chillies, ginger, onion, jaggery and salt. Bring to the boil, cover and simmer on a low heat for 30 minutes so the *dhal* is nice and soft.

2 Add the aubergine, tomatoes and drumstick, cover again and cook on a low heat for 15 minutes.

3 Meanwhile, pour the teaspoon of oil into a frying pan and add the red chilli, coriander seeds and fenugreek seeds and roast, stirring all the time, for 4–5 minutes. Grind to a fine paste with 2 tablespoons water.

4 Add the ground paste to the *dhal* and stir well. Bring to the boil.

5 Add 2 cups of water, the tamarind water and lemon juice and simmer for 10 minutes.

6 Meanwhile, pour the 2 tablespoons oil into a frying pan and fry the mustard seeds, *asafoetida* and curry leaves until the mustard seeds start to pop and splutter. Add to the pan with the teaspoon of salt and simmer for another 10 minutes, the last 5 minutes uncovered.

½ cup chana dhal, soaked
   overnight

¼ teaspoon ground turmeric

3 green chillies, finely chopped

1 tablespoon grated fresh ginger

1 onion, finely chopped

1 teaspoon grated jaggery

1 teaspoon salt

1 small aubergine (50 g/1¾ oz)
   sliced lengthways

3 fresh tomatoes, chopped

1 drumstick vegetable cut into
   8 pieces

For the paste

1 teaspoon oil

2 teaspoons dried red chilli flakes

2 teaspoons coriander seeds

1 teaspoon fenugreek seeds

1 tablespoon tamarind water
   (2.5-cm/1-inch piece block
   tamarind soaked and broken
   down in a little boiling water
   for 30 minutes)

2 teaspoons lemon juice

For the tempering

2 tablespoons oil

1 teaspoon mustard seeds

¼ teaspoon asafoetida powder

2 curry leaves

1 teaspoon salt

Sweet dosa with raspberry and blueberry mascarpone

Spring is also the season in which to celebrate our mothers on Mothering Sunday. If you're anything like me, then you spend the week before trying to find something unique as a present, failing to find anything suitable in the shops and falling back upon the trusty old favourites of flowers, chocolates and smelly designer bath products.

One Mother's Day when I was in my early teens I had managed to annoy my Mum for some reason I can't recall, probably by failing to wake up before noon as teenagers often have a habit of doing, and so decided to make a beautiful cake as a gift and to get in her good books. Like most British-Asian families, we didn't own any kitchen scales so I just guessed how much of the ingredients to put in, thinking that, as with our Indian cooking, it would be just fine. The result was a large, round, inedible rock with messy greyish-pink icing unsuccessfully disguised by wonky, bright pink iced flowers. It was so pathetic and laughable that it instantly thawed my Mum's frosty mood.

If you are contemplating cooking something for your own *mummyji*, how about these doily-like, fragile, sweet, crispy Indian pancakes made with jaggery, coconut and cardamom served with a colourful rich mascarpone studded with fresh raspberries and blueberries? Take them up with a steaming cup of hot tea and some flowers in a vase for a luxurious breakfast in bed and I'm sure you'll stay in her good books for the whole year. *Serves 4–6*

Method

1 Combine the flour, jaggery, sugar, green cardamom powder and desiccated coconut in a large bowl with a spoon. Add enough warm water until you have a batter of pouring consistency. You should have 1½ cups of batter.

2 Pour a ladleful into a heated non-stick frying pan, using a spoon to spread it out. It will not be a smooth round shape like a pancake but have edges rather like a spider's web.

3 Using a pastry brush, gently smear a little oil on the top and edges. Turn over and cook until both sides are golden and crisp – about 2 minutes on each side.

4 After you have made 4–6 (depending on how big or thick you make them), mix the mascarpone with the berries and place a dollop in the centre of each dosa and fold. Place on a plate and serve with a dusting of coconut.

1 cup rice flour

1 tablespoon grated jaggery

1 tablespoon sugar

¼ teaspoon green cardamom powder

2 tablespoons desiccated coconut, plus extra for dusting

oil for smearing

1 tub of mascarpone

1 punnet of blueberries

1 punnet of raspberries

Saffron and pistachio rasmalai

You may have heard the word *rasmalai* used in the hilarious badboy sketches in the hit comedy series *Goodness Gracious Me*, but here is the culinary sweet that inspired the slang term.

I was recently interviewed in Tooting, where a certain café sells the most amazing *rasmalai*. I couldn't pass up the opportunity of being in such close proximity, so I made an excuse for a detour. I think the journalist was rather taken aback by the slightly crazed way in which I gobbled them up. But make these once, and you will completely understand.

Rasmalai, delicate and succulent patties of sweet, fresh, steamed cream cheese, steeped in a creamy cardamom, *kewra* and rose milk syrup and topped with saffron stands and chopped pistachios is the perfect sweet to celebrate the Hindu festival of Holi.

Holi is the riotous Indian spring festival when everyone dons plain, often white, old clothes and then playfully chase each other with brightly coloured water or powder paint, as famously depicted in the Indian blockbuster *Sholay*. Yes, that's right, paintballing for the whole family, and it is a lot of fun indeed! It is intended to replicate the youthful behaviour of Lord Krishna when he would play tricks on and tease Radha and the *gopia* (milkmaids). This serves to remind Hindus that Krishna wishes for a close and personal relationship with those who worship him.

With the white of the cream cheese reflecting the purity and innocence of the season, the golden hue of the saffron embodying the warmth of spring and the pistachio resembling the first green grass and leaves, this is the perfect sweet to enjoy on such a celebratory spring occasion. *Makes 12*

Method

8 cups whole milk

3 tablespoons vinegar

6 cups water

2 cups sugar

For the milk syrup

8 cups milk

2½ tablespoons sugar

2 tablespoons rose water

few drops of kewra essence

4 green cardamoms, slightly split

3 tablespoons chopped pistachios

pinch of saffron strands, soaked
   in 3 tablespoons warm milk
   for 30 minutes

1 Pour the milk into a very large pan – bear in mind that it will boil up, so you need enough room in the pan. Stirring all the time so it doesn't stick to the bottom, bring the milk to the boil.

2 Turn down to a very low heat and add the vinegar to curdle the milk, stirring all the time. It will now be in clumps and look like clusters of snow.

3 Drain into a colander and gently rinse with clean cold water to remove the vinegar. Gently squeeze out the water.

4 Place the cream cheese in the middle of a clean cloth (a new, clean cotton tea towel will be fine), gather the four corners together, squeeze out all the water and press into a single solid shape, folding and wrapping the tea towel neatly around it, like a pillow.

5 Place on a dinner plate and place another dinner plate on top of it. Place a heavy weight, such as a large bag of sugar, on to the second plate to press down on to the cream cheese. Leave overnight.

6 Remove the cream cheese and knead well until it is a soft and smooth dough and becomes oily in your hands.

7 Place the 6 cups of water and 2 cups of sugar in a pressure cooker and bring to the boil.

8 Divide the mixture in half and, using one half, make 6 small balls – 4 cm/1½ inches in diameter – flattening them slightly.

9 Gently place the balls into the water and steam for 6 minutes. They will expand upon steaming.

10 They will be very soft and fragile so remove gently and place on to a sheet of kitchen paper to cool. Repeat with the second half of the dough.

11 Bring the milk for the milk syrup to the boil in a large pan, stirring, then simmer for 1 hour until it has been reduced to 3 cups.

12 Take off the heat and stir in the sugar, rose water, *kewra* essence and cardamoms.

13 When the milk has cooled, add the 12 cream cheese balls and top with the pistachios and saffron milk, sprinkling the saffron strands evenly over the top.

14 Refrigerate until cold and serve.

South Indian pancakes with mustard potato filling
Masala Dosa

This vegetarian treat of moreish, wafery, yellow pancakes made from *gram* and rice flour with a mild, mashed potato, mustard seed, turmeric and coriander filling originates from South India and traditionally used to be eaten by the poorer people.

    This recipe is based on the variety sold in the Diwana Restaurant on Drummond Street in London. One of Britain's oldest, and most authentic, Indian restaurants, catering originally for other Indians, Diwana has been treating customers to this favourite for decades. I was very kindly shown how to make them by their talented head chef, and I was surprised by how simple they are to make, considering how complicated I envisaged them to be. Their variety uses *besan* (*gram* flour) instead of just plain rice flour, giving a nutty flavour and a pretty yellow colour. You could always make these on Pancake Day too if you get bored of sugar and lemon. *Makes 4*

Method

1 Heat the oil in a frying pan and add the mustard seeds. When they begin to pop, add the onion. Fry until lightly golden and add the salt, turmeric, chilli, curry leaves, coriander and lemon juice. Fry for a couple of minutes.

2 Add the potatoes to the pan and mash lightly, combining well with the mixture.

3 Place the *gram* flour and rice flour with a pinch of salt in a large mixing bowl or measuring jug. Mix well with a spoon and then add enough water to make a smooth, pancake-style batter. You should have 1 cup of batter.

4 Heat a non-stick frying pan on a medium heat and pour a quarter of the batter into the pan, tilting it and using the back of a spoon to spread it out. The edges will look like a spider's web. Try to get the dosa as thin as you can.

5 Using a pastry brush, brush a little oil on the edges (the side facing upwards).

6 When the edges are brown, about 4 minutes, lift with a fish slice on to a plate, the same side facing upwards.

7 Place a few large spoonfuls of the potato filling along the middle and fold the sides over. Gently turn over on the plate.

8 Repeat until all 4 are made.

For the filling

2 tablespoons oil

1 teaspoon mustard seeds

½ onion, finely chopped

½ teaspoon salt

¼ teaspoon ground turmeric

1 green chilli, finely chopped

2 curry leaves

small handful chopped coriander

1 tablespoon lemon juice

2 potatoes (400 g/14 oz), diced, boiled and drained

For the dosas

½ cup gram flour

½ cup rice flour

pinch of salt

oil for smearing

Cashew and prawn rice

This dish is a real favourite and so unbelievably simple. You just put everything in the pan together, quickly stir-fry, add water, steam and, Bob's your *uncleji*, there you have it: a fragrant, healthy and filling all-in-one meal to enjoy with lashings of *dahi* or as an opulent accompaniment to a larger meal, which I often make for friends or myself when I am in need of some virtuous comfort food.

I've chosen these ingredients as they are so fresh, light and indicative of spring but you can play with any ingredients you like. I recently made a version with chopped avocado and toasted pine nuts and also sometimes add in small pieces of chopped mozzarella at the stage when adding the water – the cheese melts through into the rice to give an extra element of indulgence. I recommend using a non-stick pan for making this dish, and certainly if you wish to add cheese, as otherwise it will burn at the bottom of the pan. *Serves 2*

Method

2 tablespoons oil

1 teaspoon cumin seeds

½ onion thinly sliced

250 g (9 oz) cooked and peeled prawns

2 tomatoes, diced

handful of chopped coriander

½ cup cashew nuts

½ teaspoon dried red chilli flakes

½ teaspoon salt

½ cup basmati rice, rinsed with cold water

1 cup water

1 Heat the oil in a pan and add the cumin seeds.

2 When sizzling, add the onion and fry until translucent.

3 Add the prawns, tomatoes, coriander, cashews, chilli and salt and stir-fry for 30 seconds.

4 Add the rice and stir-fry for a further 30 seconds.

5 Add the water and bring to the boil. Turn the heat down very low, cover and steam for 15 minutes.

Chilli cheese parathe

I have recently gone through a rather obsessive phase with these and have been eating them at every mealtime. Although not exactly any healthier, these are just the thing when you want a change from your usual full-English for your Sunday breakfast, served up with cumin *raita* and plenty of *achaar*.

It was my *chachiji* who first introduced me to the idea of using cheese with *parathe* and this version, with crisp layers of thin butter-fried golden bread encasing a melted Cheddar cheese and green chilli filling, is about as deluxe as you can get.

A friend recently pointed out how they are a superior version of the cheese toastie, which reminded me of how much I used to love cheese toasties as a child and is probably why I love this slightly more sophisticated variety. In fact, my sister often teases me that the only two things I remember about the day she was born are a) how disappointed I was when my Dad brought her out, all wrinkly and purple, and how I told him firmly, 'That's not a proper baby, Daddy, she's ugly and horrible, take her back and get another one,' and b) that I ate cheese toasties that day. Even when I was only eight years old, food was the centre of my world.

When making these, you must use a genuine *thawa* and not a frying pan, as sometimes suggested, as you simply will not get the same results. The *thawa* is an ancient traditional Indian utensil; indeed, primitive versions have been discovered in Harrapan archeological sites, and cave paintings have been found depicting the practice of *roti* making. I don't think our ancestors would think much of using frying pans when you can get a *thawa* cheaply from any Indian shop – they are now also sold in some supermarkets. *Makes 4*

Method

Ingredients

3 cups roti flour, plus extra for dusting
water
butter
grated Cheddar
2 green chillies, finely chopped with seeds
handful of chopped coriander
garam masala
salt

1 Place the flour in a large, shallow mixing bowl. Using your hands, add water very slowly to bind the flour together. Wash your hands.

2 Knead the dough thoroughly using your knuckles, folding the dough in and turning over repeatedly. Cover and refrigerate for 30 minutes minimum.

3 Rinse the *thawa* and place on a low heat. Take a large shallow dish, fill with more *roti* flour and place on the worktop. Get a rolling pin, a large plate, a fish slice, a dinner knife, and the butter.

4 Divide the dough into 8 portions.

5 Take a portion and roll into a ball in your hands.

6 Dust the work surface with some of the flour and flatten the ball into a disc with the flat of your fingers.

7 Cup your hands and use the edges of your hands (your little finger side) to make the disc perfectly round. Flatten again with your fingers.

8 Take the rolling pin and gently roll out to form a flat round. Turn over and roll the other side.

9 Lay in the dish of flour to coat, turn over and do the same with the other side. Shake off excess flour and lay it on the work top again. Roll out, using a circular, as well as a forwards-backwards motion, to increase the size of the *paratha*, and then turn over and roll the other side. Continue this process until you have an even round *paratha* a little larger than a tea plate. It should not be too thin.

10 Put aside and roll out another ball exactly the same size.

11 Using the knife, spread a little butter on the *paratha*.

12 Top with a layer of grated Cheddar and then sprinkle with some chilli, coriander, *garam masala* and salt.

13 Carefully place the other rolled out *paratha* on top, using the palm of your hand to smooth it, on making sure that there are no creases. Use your fingers to seal the edges.

14 Carefully place the *paratha* on the centre of the *thawa*. Cook for 15 seconds.

15 Using a fish slice, gently turn it over and smear with butter. Leave for 10 seconds and turn over. Smear with butter and keep cooking and turning until golden and brown.

Lamb cutlets

Easter is one of the most important celebrations for Christians and, although it is commonly assumed that British Asians are either Hindu, Muslim or Sikh, a significant proportion are actually Christian.

Easter is, unfortunately, increasingly becoming a secular occasion during which it seems the main aim is to watch *The Wizard of Oz* or *The Sound of Music* and eat as much chocolate as possible without making yourself sick. Although I am Sikh, we have a lot of respect for Christianity in our family. My Mum, especially, has fond memories of school church visits, and I have attended and taken part in services several times. Although I did embarrass myself during one at age 11 when I performed a solo hymn in front of the altar, accompanied by a candle-holding fellow student, whose candle I rather dramatically blew out with my over energetic vocals, leaving us all in unexpected darkness.

The majority of British Asians do recognise and enjoy the Easter celebration even if they do not celebrate it religiously. Almost every British-Asian kid is treated to an egg or two!

I look back with nostalgia at the days when the Easter story was retold in various forms on television over the Easter weekend, through cartoons for children and lengthy dramas for adults. Now, television has become almost entirely de-seasonalised, with the same type of shows (now mostly reality instead of aspirational) and movies broadcast at Christmas as at Easter and no real specific programming for occasions such as Halloween any more. Hot cross buns are now available all year round and Easter bank holiday weekend has become more of an occasion to go and buy garden furniture than anything else.

One of my most memorable Easters was when I was 13 years old and we were divided into groups at school to put together an Easter presentation for assembly. My group decided upon the admittedly unorthodox idea of a rap musical where I played the starring role of Jesus in basketball trainers, white dungarees, white T-shirt and white baseball cap. It consisted of a reworking of 90s pop classics, including 'Where Are You Baby?' by Betty Boo into 'Where Are You Jesus?' by the black-dungareed and baseball-capped mourning disciples; 'I'm Doing Fine' by Jason Donovan and my solo, piano accompanied finale of Maria McKee's 'Show Me Heaven'. Not the traditional celebration I admit, but it certainly made us think about Easter, and its message in detail, even if our interpretation was a little Sister Act.

Lamb is traditionally eaten for Easter Sunday lunch, but if you want something a little more adventurous than the usual roast, try these tender cutlets of juicy, mildly spiced minced spring lamb enveloped in a layer of coriander speckled potato mash and coated with sizzling, golden breadcrumbs. Enjoy with vegetables, gravy and mint sauce or on their own as a snack with chutneys or ketchup.

Makes 4

Method

1 Preheat the oven to 200°C, Gas Mark 6.

2 Season the mashed potato with salt and pepper and add coriander. Mash well.

3 In a large bowl, combine the minced lamb, onion, ginger, garlic, salt, *garam masala*, coriander powder and green chilli with a fork until well mixed.

4 Divide the meat into four equal portions. Make four oval patties, pressing the mixture together in the palms of your hands.

5 Mould the mashed potato around the patties to coat completely.

6 Brush the patties with the egg and coat in breadcrumbs.

7 Place on to a greased baking tray, drizzle with a little oil and bake for 1 hour in the oven. Do not turn over during cooking but use a fish slice to gently push the edges back in shape if needed.

2 large baking potatoes, boiled and mashed (with no butter or milk)

salt and pepper to season

handful of chopped coriander

250 g (9 oz) minced lamb

½ onion, grated

1 teaspoon grated fresh ginger

1 clove garlic, crushed

½ teaspoon salt

½ teaspoon garam masala

1 teaspoon coriander powder

½ green chilli, finely chopped

1 egg, beaten

100 g (3½ oz) breadcrumbs

oil

Pan-fried baby potatoes with cumin and mint

These whole baby potatoes are silkily soft on the inside and encrusted with fried cumin and mint on the outside. They are so simple to make and are an unusual accompaniment to a traditional Easter lunch or indeed any Sunday lunch roast. Thinking of Sunday lunch reminds me of an endearing story once told to me by a journalist. While discussing British culinary traditions that British Asians have adopted, she told me about a British-Asian friend of hers, whose parents were of South Indian origin. When they arrived here, one of the first things the mother observed was the traditional roast lunch where Yorkshire pudding was served. Thinking it was an essential part of every British meal, this lovely lady set about determinedly serving Yorkshire pudding with every meal in her household. Therefore a typical supper during the journalist's friend's youth would be *dhal* and Yorkshire pudding until the mother realised much later on that it was not the done thing to serve Yorkshire pudding with everything, as she had very sweetly thought for years. *Serves 4*

Method

1   Boil the potatoes whole in their skins for about 12 minutes until tender. Drain and set aside.

2   Heat the oil in a large frying pan and add the cumin seeds. Once they begin to sizzle, add the *garam masala*, potatoes and salt. Stir-fry until the potatoes are golden and crisp.

3   Stir in the mint, fry for another 30 seconds and serve.

750 g (1 lb 10 oz) small or salad potatoes

3 tablespoons olive oil

3 teaspoons cumin seeds

½ teaspoon garam masala

good sprinkle of salt

handful of finely chopped fresh mint leaves

Rice with mung beans *Khichidi*

This is a wholesome, nourishing, risotto-style dish of rice cooked with mung beans and then laced with butter, *asafoetida*, cumin and cassia bark. It is often used to fortify those who are feeling a little under the weather and is just the thing on a blustery, showery spring afternoon. It is best eaten with *dahi*, some *achaar* and plenty of feel-good TV.

You might recognise the name as being similar to the name of the Anglo-Indian breakfast dish 'kedgeree'. *Khichidi* is the traditional Indian dish that was adopted by the colonial British who added the fried fish they often ate for breakfast and, over time, the British mercantile invention of curry powder, renaming it kedgeree after their pronunciation.

In fact, there are many English terms and words that have their roots in Indian ones, such as 'cup of chaa', chutney, pyjamas, veranda, cot, bungalow, pukka, dungarees, jodhpurs, khaki, loot, punch (as in the drink), and thug. The English word juggernaut for a gigantic lorry or an object or force that crushes all in its path, for example, derives from Hindu religious terminology: Jagannath (a title of the god Vishnu) is the Hindu lord of the universe and, in homage to the imagery of him on a chariot, towering chariots are built and paraded along the streets in a procession for the festival of Ratha Yatra. *Serves 4*

Method

1 Place the *dhal* and rice in a pan with 2 cups of water, the salt and the turmeric. Stir, bring to the boil and then cover and cook on a low heat for 15 minutes.

2 Meanwhile, heat the oil in a frying pan and add the remaining ingredients, apart from the butter. Fry until the onion is golden.

3 Pour on to the cooked *dhal* and rice and stir gently. Add a good knob of butter and let it melt on top.

½ cup moong dhal, soaked overnight and rinsed

½ cup washed rice

1 teaspoon salt

¼ teaspoon ground turmeric

2 tablespoons oil

large pinch of asafoetida

1 teaspoon cumin seeds

1 green chilli, finely chopped

½ onion, finely sliced

1 stick cassia bark

butter

Potatoes and fresh peas
Aloo Mattar

This is one of my favourite *sabjia* and I have wonderful memories of sitting as a child at the table shelling peas while chatting, whether at my house or that of relatives. The result is a fresh, clean flavoured *sabji*, with plenty of clear *thari* (sauce), bursting with bouncy sweet peas and soft potatoes, best enjoyed with simple *roti*, *dahi* and *achaar* or Mini Mint *Parathe* (page 89).

This simple *sabji* made with long-awaited spring peas, bursting from their full, green pods, is ideal to make for Langar or at home for the Indian festival of Baisakhi, which is particularly celebrated by Punjabis. This occasion celebrates the beginning of the farming season and vigorous *bhangra* dancers often relay agricultural tales. This day is also of significance to Buddhists as Buddha attained enlightenment and nirvana on this auspicious day.

Baisakhi is one of the most crucial dates on the Sikh calendar as it is also the occasion that celebrates the momentous day in 1699 when the tenth Guru, Guru Gobind Singh Ji founded the Sikh Brotherhood – the Khalsa – giving the identity of the 'Singh' to the Sikh community, which extended to the wearing of the five 'Ks' to mark them as distinct. It is therefore a popular time for holding the Amrit ceremony, which is held for those who wish to become full members of the religion. It is also the day on which it is believed Guru Nanak Dev Ji set out on his missionary travels. It is furthermore regarded as the Sikh New Year.

Baisakhi 1919 was also the date of the Jallianwala Bagh Massacre. General Dyer ignorantly, and conveniently, perceived the gathering to be a political meeting and ordered his troops to open fire. Therefore Baisakhi today is a very important religious, social, seasonal and political occasion. *Serves 4–6*

Method

1 Heat the oil in a large pan and add the onion and garlic. Fry until golden brown.

2 Remove the pan from the heat for a few seconds and then add the tomato, ginger, chillies, salt, turmeric, *garam masala* and half the coriander. Cook on a low heat until the mixture becomes shiny and the oil separates out.

3 Add the peas, turn up the heat and stir-fry for 1 minute. Add the potatoes and continue to stir-fry for a couple of minutes so that the potatoes and peas are well covered.

4 Add 2½ cups of boiling water. Bring to the boil, cover and simmer for 20 minutes. Sprinkle with the remaining coriander.

2 tablespoons + 1 teaspoon oil

1 large onion, finely chopped

1 clove garlic, finely chopped

1 cup canned chopped tomatoes whizzed in a blender with ½ cup water

2 teaspoons grated fresh ginger

2 green chillies, finely chopped

1 teaspoon salt

1 teaspoon ground turmeric

3 teaspoons garam masala

2 handfuls of chopped coriander

450 g (1 lb) fresh peas in pods to give 2 cups fresh shelled peas or 2 cups frozen peas

3 potatoes, peeled and chopped into small chunks

Mini coconut spring rolls

These tiny bite-sized rolls of flaky pastry crammed with sweet, moist coconut filling are wonderful hot or cold and can be eaten as little snacks on their own or served as a dessert by stacking several on a plate and serving with ice cream.

Coconut is used widely in Indian food, mostly in its milk form in South Indian savoury dishes and in its desiccated form for the majority of Indian sweets. In its whole form it is also vastly important as an auspicious symbol and features in many religious and social occasions. It replaced animal sacrifice when India largely became vegetarian, so, instead of blood being spilt, the coconut is often smashed upon the ground. When I was a child I would look on in fascination at brides who could not get up from being seated on the *gurudwara* floor during the wedding eremony, despite attempts to hoist them up by their sisters and cousins, due to the sheer weight of decorated coconut shells hanging from both wrists. *Makes 28*

Method

1 Preheat the oven to 200°C, Gas Mark 6.

2 Heat the butter in a pan on a low heat. When melted, add the coconut and toast by stirring continuously until golden.

3 Switch off the heat and allow the pan to cool a little before adding the sugar. Stir well and then add the evaporated milk. Stir thoroughly so that you have a nice, moist coconut mixture. Place in a bowl and allow to cool.

4 Cut each filo pastry sheet in half, lengthways. With a sharp knife and a clean ruler, cut rectangles of 9.5 x 10.5 cm (3¾ x 4¼ inches). You should be able to cut 28 complete rectangles, with no tears or cuts, out of the pastry.

5 Making sure that the remaining rectangles are kept covered with cling film, take a rectangle and place on a flat board or the worktop with the side measuring 9.5 cm (3¾ inches) nearest to you.

6 Brush the edges very lightly with oil and, using your fingers, place a small amount of filling mixture on the rectangle at the end nearest to you, being sure to leave a gap of 1-cm (½-inch) from the end nearest to you and on either side. Using your fingers, shape the mixture into a sausage shape.

7 Fold the outside edges in and lightly press on to the mixture to secure. Holding the edges, roll up the 1 cm (½-inch) edge nearest to you on to the filling and then finish rolling, using a little oil to secure the seal.

8 Place all the rolls on an oiled baking sheet, seal side down, and brush each lightly with oil.

9 Bake for 15 minutes in the centre of the oven.

2 tablespoons butter

1 cup desiccated coconut

2½ teaspoons sugar

⅓ cup evaporated milk

270 g packet – 6 sheets – Jus-Rol frozen, uncooked filo pastry, defrosted

vegetable oil

Cardamom and gold
chocolate truffles

My parents, like most other British-Asian parents, instilled in me the value of working hard to achieve in life. As part of a generation who were often skilled or educated back in their motherland of India, they found themselves victims of insults, abuse, prejudice and discrimination as immigrants.

There were men who were doctors in India who suddenly found themselves working in biscuit factories to earn a measly wage while women who had only known purdah found themselves cleaning the toilet bowls of strangers.

The degrees of experience differed, but one thing was unquestionable. When these parents talked of working hard to achieve in life, they were not simply referring to educational success or financial prosperity alone. They were referring to a means by which to achieve respect, dignity, to be seen as equals and to achieve self-sufficiency.

So, when the young British Asian I mentioned Fairtrade to last week said, 'Oh, I've heard of that, it's one of those white, middle-class, do-gooder issues, isn't it?', I said the following: We are a previously subjugated people, the colonisation of whom was rooted in trade. As a people who have fought and laboured for rights, success, progress and material comfort, I believe that we should have empathy with and a moral responsibility towards those who are only asking for that very same right: to be able to work to achieve. To provide for their families, feed their children, invest in their countries and environment, work their way out of debt and poverty – to simply hold their heads high. They do not want charity, simply a fair wage for their hard work. It is very easy to become desensitised and dismiss the issue, to view it as something that happens 'over there' to 'those people' who live in 'those countries'.

Imagine if it were you. If you had spent hours toiling under the baking sun to be paid less than the cost of working in the first place. And imagine if the human cost was to see your child die because you simply could not feed him, no matter how hard you worked. Imagine seeing a consumer put down a packet of Fairtrade tea bags because they cost just 10 pence more, knowing that that 10 pence could have gone towards saving your child's life. It sounds a barbaric system when you apply it to yourself.

There are many issues we cannot directly contribute towards in this world – this is not one of them. What is so empowering about Fairtrade is that each one of us has the potential to directly affect the lives and welfare of these people every day, and get something delicious, or beautiful in the case of Fairtrade roses, out of it too.

It almost seems too easy to be true. But it is. Your consumer and commercial choices have an enormous impact and they will also benefit the global economy and contribute to international peace and security.

If these rich, decadent truffles made with cream, chocolate and cardamom then dusted with glittering edible gold dust, don't tempt you to use some Fairtrade chocolate, then I don't know what will. Go on, indulge yourself, give a boxful to friends and do a little good in the process. *Makes 30 large truffles*

Method

200 ml double cream

1 teaspoon green cardamom powder

300 g (10½ oz) Fairtrade plain chocolate, chopped

250 g (9 oz) Fairtrade plain chocolate, melted

50 g (1½ oz) sweet cocoa powder

edible gold glitter

1 Place the cream and the cardamom powder in a saucepan and gently bring to the boil on a low heat, stirring continuously. Remove from the heat.

2 In a heat-proof bowl, pour the cream over the chopped chocolate.

3 Stir until melted and then leave to cool at room temperature for about 30 minutes.

4 Beat with a wooden spoon for about 5 minutes until thick.

5 Using a teaspoon, scoop up an amount and quickly shape into a rough ball/nugget shape and set down on a sheet of greaseproof paper on a tray – you have to be quick with this as the chocolate will melt upon contact with your hands.

6 Refrigerate for about 20 minutes until firm.

7 Dip each truffle briefly in the melted chocolate and then place back on the greaseproof paper.

8 When you have done this to all the truffles, dust each with the cocoa powder and then with a little of the gold glitter.

9 Place on a plate and either serve or refrigerate.

South Indian steamed rice cakes *Idli*

South Indians are generally rice eaters, as opposed to Punjabis who gain their carbohydrate intake from wheat *rotia*, and they are extremely inventive with its uses. These light, plainly flavoured rounds that resemble little moons are made from a mixture of ground rice and ground *urid dhal*, which is fermented and then steamed in moulds until they form small airy sponges. They are most commonly eaten for breakfast, although I think they are a fantastic weekend brunch food or teatime snack.

As they are so plain, they are traditionally served with both *sambhar* (a vegetable and lentil broth, see page 34) and fresh coconut chutney (see page 91) into which pieces of broken *idli* are dipped, but only with the right hand, the left hand is considered unclean to most Indians (I'll spare you from going into why!).

It is also likely that the western term 'curry' for all types of Indian food – a generic term I highly despise – may have evolved from the South Indian Tamil word *kari*. *Kari* means black pepper and was an entirely appropriate term for spicy accompaniments, such as *sambhar*. This term originated in the days when dishes were made with black pepper to add fiery flavour, as this was before the chilli was introduced to India. However, the anglicised word 'curry' was later used to denote any Indian dish from any region and of any consistency or flavour. *Makes 18*

Method

1 Soak the *urid dhal* and rice separately in water overnight.

2 Grind together with 2–3 tablespoons water to make a smooth batter, like cake mixture.

3 Place the mixture in a bowl, cover with kitchen paper and place in a warm place, such as an airing cupboard, for 8 hours.

4 Add the salt and stir well into the mixture.

5 Place 2½ cups of water in a large wok and bring to the boil. Place a steaming-ring in the wok, making sure it doesn't touch the water, and place a metal egg poacher, greased with oil, on the ring to warm it up. My egg poacher steams three *idlis* at a time.

6 On a medium heat, pour the batter into the moulds until two-thirds full.

7 Cover with the wok lid, so completely sealed, and steam for 15 minutes.

8 Cool before removing from the moulds and making a next batch.

9 Serve with coconut chutney and *sambhar*.

½ cup urid dhal

½ cup rice

water

½ teaspoon salt

a little oil

Date chutney

Dates are commonly used in desserts but this powerful, thick, hot, spicy, sticky chutney with sweet undertones shows just how versatile they can be. It is very easy to make and can be kept in the refrigerator for up to a week. The dates are ground down into a single tacky mass in a grinder and then heated in a pan with tamarind, jaggery, garlic, ginger, lime and chilli, stirring all the time to melt down and bind the ingredients together.

It has many uses. You can use it to accompany traditional *sabjia* and *roti*, but it is also great with a roast lunch (especially with roast potatoes), with *samose*, stirred into hot, plain basmati rice with a little butter, with a ploughman's lunch and with chicken in tortilla wraps. *Makes a jarful*

Method

50 g (1¾ oz) block tamarind

1 cup boiling water

20 fresh pitted dates, ground in a mini-blender or grinder

45 g (1¾ oz) grated jaggery

2 cloves garlic, crushed

1 teaspoon fresh grated ginger

squeeze of lime

¼ teaspoon salt

¼ teaspoon red chilli powder

sprigs of mint to garnish

1 Place the tamarind in a bowl with the boiling water and leave to soak for a few minutes. Using a wooden spoon, gently break up the tamarind in the water, stirring gently to help it dissolve. Leave for 10 minutes.

2 Pour the tamarind water through a tea-strainer into another bowl, pushing through as much of the solids as possible with the back of a spoon.

3 Place 1 cup of the tamarind water in a saucepan on a low heat.

4 Add the remaining ingredients, except for the mint, and stir continuously for about 5 minutes until it is all dissolved and well blended.

5 Leave to cool and then serve garnished with mint. Store in the fridge.

Cumin raita

This traditional mildly spiced yogurt accompaniment, which my friends rave about, can literally transform the taste of the rest of the meal. Roasted, wood-scented cumin is pounded then added to fresh, cool yogurt with tomato, cucumber and onion, finally sprinkled with a dusting of *garam masala* and red chilli. It goes with, and is a key component of, just about every Indian meal. You can also try it on top of jacket potatoes too as a healthy topping or even as a salad dressing or dip. Really watch the cumin though when it is in the pan, as it can burn very quickly. *Serves 4–6*

Method

1 Heat a dry non-stick frying pan and add the cumin seeds. Dry roast them, stirring with a wooden spoon all the time, for a few minutes until they become darker and release a woody aroma – do not let them burn! Bash in a pestle and mortar.

2 In a large bowl, mix the yogurt with enough milk to make quite a runny yogurt.

3 Add the tomatoes, cucumber, onion, salt and crushed cumin seeds and stir well.

4 Decorate with sprinkles of *garam masala* and red chilli powder. Finish with sprigs of coriander.

1 tablespoon cumin seeds

500 ml (18 fl oz) set natural low-fat yogurt

milk

2 tomatoes, diced

¼ cucumber, diced

¼ red onion, very finely chopped

sprinkle of salt

sprinkle of garam masala

sprinkle of red chilli powder

coriander sprigs

Apricot and almond milk

This luxurious milkshake is reminiscent of rich Mughal flavourings and is an extravagant, regal version of the humble milkshake, best served in cut-glass tumblers over ice.

Sweet whole almonds are soaked in water overnight, then ground to a paste to be whizzed and frothed up with fleshy apricots, sugar syrup, cold milk and creamy vanilla ice cream. *Serves 4*

Method

100 g (3½ oz) sweet almonds, soaked in water overnight

227 g (8 oz) can of apricot halves in syrup

2½ cups cold milk

10 tablespoons vanilla ice cream

1 Grind the almonds to a paste.

2 In a drinks blender, add the almonds and all remaining ingredients and whiz until frothy.

3 Serve topped with a little extra ice cream.

Mint lassi

Mum (my nan, we all call her Mum) used to grow big bucketfuls of fresh mint in the back garden. The scent was so strong and invigorating from those bristly leaves that it would overpower the whole garden where we played as children. Whenever I smell mint leaves, it always takes me back to memories of running, dodging the washing line, around that garden.

Lassis are an extremely popular Indian drink, often made at the table by briskly stirring some yogurt from the meal into a tumbler of water. Here, mint is used to enliven the traditional *lassi* and is perfect with chilli cheese *parathe* for breakfast or simply savoured on its own. *Serves 1*

Method

1 glass of water

3 tablespoons natural set low-fat yogurt

8 mint leaves

pinch of cumin powder

large pinch of salt

sprig of mint

Whizz all the ingredients in a blender and serve over ice. Garnish with mint.

Blood orange sharbart

With increasingly unpredictable weather as a result of global warming, we can experience anything from hail, snow, thunder or baking sun during our spring season now. Make the most of a warm, sunny day out in the garden with this fun, quirky, refreshing crushed ice dessert that is similar to a Slush Puppy. This palate-cleansing sweet, made with fresh blood oranges, rose water and cinnamon and decorated with slices of juicy star fruit, is best served with both a straw and a spoon. *Serves 2*

Method

1 Place the orange juice, sugar, ice cubes, rose water and cinnamon into a drinks blender and whiz until the ice is roughly crushed.

2 Pour the mixture into a freezer bag and freeze for 30 minutes.

3 Divide the orange slices between two dessert glasses. Take the bag out of the freezer and bash with a rolling pin to crush.

4 Divide between the glasses on top of the purée.

5 Decorate with the star fruit slices and the mint.

3$\frac{1}{2}$ cups of freshly squeezed blood orange juice

2 tablespoons sugar

4 ice cubes

2 teaspoons rose water

1 teaspoon ground cinnamon

1 blood orange, peeled and cut into thin slices

4 slices of star fruit

2 sprigs of mint

The sultry temperature sizzles,

Heat charring succulent meat and fruits of the sea,

The zesty aroma of chilli, garlic, ginger, lemongrass, mint, cumin and
coriander spicing the silky cyan sky,

The sun lowers its gaze, dipping its glare to the deepest papaya glow,

Summer lays down amid the palm trees,

Looking up at the indigo chiffon,

Perfumed with pineapple and coconut, jasmine and jacaranda...

Green masala roast chicken breasts

Summer is all about lazy days spent in the garden with your nearest and dearest and a barbecue. Although we didn't have a barbecue when I was little, my Dad was always marinating and roasting meats under the grill, much to the envy of neighbours who would smell the aroma wafting over the fence. Instead of the usual hot dog and hamburger fare, try these chicken breasts marinated in a mixture of yogurt with coriander leaves, green chillies, cracked coriander seeds, garlic and ginger to give a char-grilled muted green crust. Serve with salad, potatoes, chips, or in pitta pockets with cumin *raita* or a slice of cheese.
Serves 4

Method

4 green chillies

1 teaspoon ground turmeric

2 tablespoons whole coriander seeds

handful of chopped coriander

2 teaspoons garam masala

6 cloves garlic

1 small onion, roughly chopped

1 tablespoon grated ginger (not frozen)

1 tablespoon natural yogurt

2 tablespoons lemon juice

4 tablespoons mild and light olive oil

1 teaspoon salt

4 chicken breasts, skinned and scored with a knife

1 Preheat the oven to 200°C, Gas Mark 6.

2 Place all the ingredients, except the chicken, in a blender or grinder and whizz to a thick paste. Massage the chicken with the paste, cover and marinate in the fridge for at least 4 hours or overnight.

3 Shake off any excess marinade and place the chicken breasts on a baking sheet. Roast for 30 minutes, turning over halfway through. Alternatively, barbeque.

Tandoori tuna steak

They say fish is brain food so what better dish to enjoy during the dreaded exam season than these thick, ruby red, tuna steaks steeped in a tasty marinade. Grill or barbecue them to your liking and enjoy with chips and coconut chutney, taking your mind off revising for a few minutes to recharge.

As in the majority of British-Asian families, academic achievement was extremely important in mine as a means by which to secure a successful career. I once asked my Dad when I was quite young why I, and my siblings, were given English first names rather than Indian ones. I didn't expect the answer I received. He explained in a matter-of-fact manner that he thought we would stand a better chance of having our job applications and CVs not automatically tossed in the bin by employers if we had English first names. Nice to know that Dad was already thinking ahead. I was very lucky too, considering my Dad went on to tell me that the other names they had shortlisted for me were Margaret, Barbara and Vivien.

In a weird way, I've always rather enjoyed exams but my most bizarre exam experience occured during my GCSE German speaking examination, for which I was particularly nervous. German, like Punjabi, and unlike English, has a polite form and, for some reason, my nerves went into overdrive, habit kicked in and on some sort of autopilot mode, I actually replied *hanji* a good few times instead of answering *ja* – the Punjabi instead of German word for 'yes' – as I would at home when speaking the polite form. The most remarkable thing was that I got an A grade – they must have thought I was speaking some form of advanced German, as I answered with such conviction.

Hindu students pray to the elephant god Ganesh before exams, as he is the remover of obstacles. This is also interesting as elephants in India are traditionally depended upon to remove obstacles such as fallen tree trunks in the road. *Serves 2*

Method

1 Combine all the ingredients in a bowl, apart from the tuna, to make a marinade.

2 Place the tuna steaks in the marinade and gently massage the marinade in for a few seconds. Making sure the steaks are completely covered in marinade, cover and refrigerate for 4 hours at least.

3 Shake off excess and grill to your own preference.

2 ruby red firm tuna steaks without skin or bone, about 240 g (8½ oz)

½ cup natural low-fat set yogurt

1 clove garlic, crushed

1 teaspoon grated fresh ginger

1 teaspoon coriander seeds, crushed in a pestle and mortar

¼ teaspoon salt

1 teaspoon tandoori masala

¼ teaspoon dried red chilli flakes

squeeze of lemon juice

½ teaspoon oil

few sprigs of mint, finely chopped

Prawn puri

Endless childhood summers were always peppered with ritual annual trips to Alton Towers, Drayton Manor and Marketon or Wollaton Park. And whether they were enjoyed as a nuclear family or with our extended relatives, there was one reassuringly constant factor – the food. The car boot was always heaving with Tupperware boxes filled with assorted *sabjia*, meat dishes, *dahi*, salads and *achaars* with *pooria* and *parathe* wrapped in foil, served up with plastic glasses full of fizzy Coca-Cola, limeade or cherryade, while we batted away inquisitive flies with *chunnia* or pieces of kitchen paper. We would find a spot on which to lay our trusty tartan blanket and spread out our feast, which I'm sure for some of the elders, was the highlight of the outing. While keeping an eye out for playful unrestrained dogs that I was convinced would bolt towards me to take a chunk out of my calf at the first available opportunity and while non-Asian families sniggered, making me slightly self-conscious, I would sit there under the sun, thankful deep down that I was eating such delights and not soggy white bread cheese and tomato sandwiches. Prawn *pooria* make for perfect summer picnic food with juicy prawns stirred into a sweet and sour tomato, cumin and tamarind sauce, scooped up with deep-fried *pooria*. *Serves 4*

Method

1 Heat the oil in a pan and add the cumin seeds. When sizzling, add the onion and garlic and fry until quite a deep golden brown.

2 Remove the pan from the heat for a few seconds and add the canned tomatoes, salt, *garam masala*, turmeric, chillies, ginger, sugar, coriander and 7 tablespoons of the tamarind water. Cook on a low to medium heat until the mixture becomes shiny and the oil separates out.

3 Add the prawns, turn up the heat and stir-fry them in the sauce very quickly, just to heat through. Do not cook for too long as then water will start to emerge from the prawns.

4 When heated through, stir in the diced tomatoes and switch off the heat.

Pooria deep-fried bread Take 2 cups roti flour and some oil, for deep-frying. Make the dough in exactly the same way as for roti (page 25). As with roti, but using smaller balls, roll out smaller, saucer-sized rotis. Make them slightly thicker than roti. Heat the oil to about 170°C or until a little piece of dough rises to the surface. Deep-fry the pooria until they are puffed up and brown. Drain on kitchen paper.

2 tablespoons oil

2 teaspoons cumin seeds

1 onion, thinly sliced

2 cloves garlic, finely chopped

⅓ cup canned chopped tomatoes, whizzed in a blender

1 teaspoon salt

2 teaspoons garam masala

½ teaspoon ground turmeric

2 green chillies, finely chopped

1 teaspoon grated fresh ginger

1 teaspoon sugar

handful of chopped coriander

2.5-cm (1-inch) square of block tamarind, soaked, and broken up in ⅔ cup boiling water for 40 minutes

500 g (1 lb 2 oz) peeled and cooked prawns

2 fresh tomatoes, diced

Punjabi fish and chips

There is a rather pathetic misconception that British Asians never eat anything but Indian food. I'm certainly not the only one who was annoyingly teased with the typical comment 'Bet you only eat curry' while waiting in the school canteen queue as a kid. Although I obviously enjoyed a wealth of Indian food at home, I also ate pizza, chips, fish fingers and crisps too, like everyone else, and spent my entire childhood trying to prove that by rather forcefully inviting friends home for tea. And the older generation are also very partial to their British culinary favourites. One of my Dad's most favourite foods in the world is good old fish and chips, which he frequently orders whenever he gets the chance, often with a side portion of mushy peas. So if your dad is anything like mine and enjoys fish and chips with a beer, then this spicy version, with carom seeds and three types of chilli, in a golden batter dished up with chips sprinkled with *garam masala*, is just the thing to treat your dad to on Father's Day. *Serves 2*

Method

400 g (14 oz) cod fillet, skinned
and cut into large pieces

salt and pepper

½ cup self-raising flour, plus
extra to dust

¼ cup gram flour

small handful of chopped
coriander

1 tablespoon lemon juice

½ teaspoon ajwain seeds

½ teaspoon grated fresh ginger

1 garlic clove, crushed

1 teaspoon salt

1 teaspoon garam masala

¼ teaspoon dried red chilli flakes

1 green chilli, finely chopped

¼ teaspoon red chilli powder

3 large potatoes, cut into chips

garam masala, to season

2 wedges of lime

1 Season the fish with the salt and pepper and dust with self-raising flour.

2 In a large bowl, combine the self-raising flour and *gram* flour with enough water to make a smooth, thick batter.

3 Add the remaining ingredients except the *garam masala* and lime to the batter and mix well.

4 Dip the cod pieces into the batter and deep-fry at about 170°C for approximately 8 minutes until crisp and golden.

5 Fry the chips until golden and dust with salt and *garam masala*.

6 Serve the Punjabi fish and chips with the lime wedges and some mayonnaise.

Mango, rocket, red onion and vine tomato salad

This light, fresh salad, which only takes minutes to toss, is the perfect summer salad and is an unusual accompaniment to barbecued meats, fish and kebabs. The mango is a popular Indian fruit and works very well in this salad with its dense sweetness searing into the savoury flavours.

If you are lucky enough to come across any at an Indian shop, you should also try the smaller 'sucking' mangoes. My older relatives have fond childhood memories of eating these mangos in India by making a hole in the top and sucking out the juice.

Buddhists also consider the mango sacred as the Buddha was accustomed to retire in a mango grove – a pure white mango tree sprouted from the ground at the spot where the Buddha planted a mango stone and ran water over his hands. *Serves 4*

Method

1 Place all ingredients in a large salad bowl and toss.
2 Sprinkle with *garam masala*.

1 large ripe mango, peeled and
    cut into long, thin slices

1 bag of rocket leaves

1 red onion, finely sliced

1 packet vine cherry tomatoes,
    still on the vine but snipped
    into small sections

handful of torn fresh mint leaves

extra virgin olive oil

coarsely ground black pepper,
    to taste

lemon juice

sprinkle of garam masala

Simple boneless chicken

Every couple of years, the nation is gripped with footie mania over the summer, with many an England fan visiting Indian restaurants after matches for lager, a *vindaloo* and patriotic banter. Some of my female friends are very much into football, regularly attending and watching matches on television, and, although there are a great deal of non-Asian girls in Britain who cannot stand football, my friends really couldn't understand why I took no interest in and had such little experience or knowledge of it. They found it weird that while football was a huge part of their youth and upbringing, it had completely passed me by. Their youth involved football being played on television over the weekend, with shouts and yelps emerging from the living room. There were trips to matches with their fathers to be enjoyed, all wrapped up in their glorious team scarves and hats, like ancient tribal markings. They could not get to grips with why I knew so little about it: 'But you're British!' they would exclaim.

The explanation is really quite simple. When I was growing up, there was enough racism to deal with on a daily basis as it was. My Dad was not exactly going to say to his young children, 'Come along now kids, wrap up warm, we're going for a day out to the football, where we can watch the team play a great game and then listen to stocky skinheads shout expletives and racist slurs at us while aiming bottles and empty beer cans at our heads.' Football was simply seen as racist, violent and dangerous. The word equated yob culture and hooliganism and we were strongly advised to keep well away from it.

However, like many of the younger generation, my brother Aneil is an avid fan of all sports. He got into football during his teens and is a die-hard fan of Manchester United. For a recent Christmas present, I bought VIP tickets for my brother, my Dad and I to go and watch Manchester United play Charlton at Old Trafford. For my brother, it was nothing short of a dream come true. It was the first time any of us had been to a football match and we had a truly memorable time. During the pre-match meal, my Dad explained what a shame it was that he had never felt able to attend a football match in this country, after enjoying playing football so much as a child in India. I was speechless. Apart from the hooligan factor, I thought the other reason why we did not embrace football as a family was because my Dad had no interest in it. I was so saddened to learn that a genuine love of the sport was prematurely stunted by the mindless antics of those who had no better release for their social frustration.

Thankfully, there is now zero-tolerance towards this form of activity. As football and Indian food often go hand in hand, why not try something different from the *vindaloos* and *phaals* and instead enjoy this home-made traditional chicken dish this year? Succulent pieces of chicken are coated in plenty of rich, deep sauce and it goes perfectly with rice. So add more chillies to make it as hot as you like it, put a few beers in the fridge, hang your St George's flag (who was actually a Palestinian) outside your window and cheer to your heart's content. *Serves 4*

Method

1 Heat the oil in a pan with the cumin seeds, cloves and bay leaf. When the seeds are sizzling, add the onion and garlic. Cover and cook on a very low heat for 10 minutes.

2 Switch off the heat. Remove the bay leaf and cloves and discard. Using a slotted spoon, transfer the onion and cumin into a blender or grinder and whiz until smooth, leaving the oil in the pan.

3 Put the pan with the oil back on the heat and, when hot, add the blended onion. Fry until golden brown. Remove the pan from the heat for a few seconds and add the tomatoes, chilli, ginger, salt, *garam masala*, turmeric and chopped coriander. Add a splash of water and cook on a low heat, stirring.

4 When the mixture is shiny and the oil has separated, add the chicken. Turn up the heat and stir-fry for a few minutes to coat thoroughly.

5 Add enough water to just cover the chicken and bring to the boil. Cover and simmer for 20 minutes. Remove the lid, turn up the heat, and cook for a further 5 minutes until you have a nice, rich, thick sauce.

6 Garnish with the coriander.

⅓ cup oil

1 teaspoon cumin seeds

2 cloves

1 bay leaf

1 onion, roughly chopped

2 garlic cloves, roughly chopped

½ cup canned chopped tomatoes,
    whizzed in a blender

2 green chillies, finely chopped

1 teaspoon grated fresh ginger

1½ teaspoons salt

1½ teaspoons garam masala

1 teaspoon ground turmeric

handful of chopped coriander

450 g (1 lb) diced boneless
    chicken breast, washed

coriander sprigs

Hot chickpea salad

I love the Middle Eastern quality of this salad which takes minutes to make and is fantastic eaten hot straight away but is equally good as picnic food. Simple, buttery chickpeas are stir-fried with a heady, perfumed concoction of red onion, olive oil, garlic, nutmeg, cinnamon, chilli, lemon and coriander, then mixed with spring onion and tomato for an exotic combination best served with toasted pitta, yogurt and pickled chillies.

To make the toasted pitta, cut into and around the edges of a pitta, so you have two leaves, then cut across diagonally into strips. Mix together in a bowl a little melted butter, a clove of crushed garlic, a squeeze of lime and some dried coriander leaves. Brush this over the pitta strips and grill until both sides are lightly brown. *Serves 1–2*

Method

2 teaspoons mild olive oil

¼ red onion, thinly sliced

2 cloves of garlic, finely chopped

1 can chickpeas, drained

salt and pepper, to season

pinch of ground nutmeg

½ teaspoon cinnamon powder

¼ teaspoon red chilli powder

generous dash of lemon juice

small handful of chopped
    coriander

1 spring onion, finely chopped

1 tomato, finely chopped

1 Heat the oil in a pan and add the onion and garlic. When softened, add the chickpeas and stir-fry lightly for a couple of minutes, adding all the remaining ingredients apart from the spring onion and tomato.

2 Remove from the heat and toss with the spring onion and tomato.

Lemon and lime rice

Summer is all about bright, juicy ingredients and this citrus-flavoured rice is full of sunshine. Colourful shavings of fragrant zest and the zingy, abundant juice of seasonal lemons and limes are added to basmati rice. Serve it hot with a smoky meat dish or chill and mix with toasted almonds, feta cheese, thin strips of baby spinach and roasted cherry tomatoes for a great salad to take on a trip to the seaside or to perhaps enjoy at a summer street party.

The best summer party for me has to be the street party held for the Golden Jubilee celebration in 2002. That whole summer was filled with patriotic pride, especially amongst the British-Asian community, who were proud to be British and of their contribution to British society and history. Indians were captivated by the Royal Family during colonial rule, being particularly fond of Queen Victoria, and many dreamt of visiting Buckingham Palace on their arrival in Britain during the 1960s. The fascination with this institution, which seemed to represent so much of the attractive side of England to Indians, has very much remained alive in the decades since. The Silver Jubilee condiment stand at my grandparents' (*Papiji* and *Bibiji*) house, diligently kept shiny, was the central feature of the dining table, precariously balancing salt and pepper pots upon it. For the Golden Jubilee party, for which my *Phupherji*, *Pooiji*, and cousins Sunny and Sukhmanie drove to Norfolk from Walsall, rows of tables were aligned along our cul-de-sac and each family brought out their culinary offerings. We provided *samose*, freshly fried by my Mum, and other treats to go along with the pasta, crisps, rice salads, sandwiches, sausage rolls, chicken and cakes which overflowed the table. The atmosphere of unity, celebration and good cheer was unrivalled as we played three-legged, sack and egg-and-spoon races (which my Mum got quite competitive about, having been very sporty at school). As I gazed out at the fuschia-streaked sunset sky, the sound of laughter wafting through the warm air and glasses clinking as my Father regaled the neighbours, still relaxing outside, with amusing tales, basking in the nostalgic spirit of the day, I spied the first of the evening's many glorious fireworks in the distance and felt overwhelmingly proud to be British. *Serves 2*

Method

1 Heat the oil in a pan and add the lemon and lime zest.

2 Fry on a low heat for a couple of seconds and then add the lemon and lime juice and salt and pepper.

3 Add the washed rice and turn up the heat to medium. Stir-fry the rice for about a minute.

4 Add the water and bring to the boil. When it is boiling, reduce the heat to very low, cover and simmer for 10–12 minutes.

5 Garnish with mint.

1 tablespoon oil

zest and juice of 1 lemon

zest and juice of 2 limes

grind of salt

grind of pepper

1 cup basmati rice, washed

2 cups of water

mint leaves, to garnish

Corn cobettes

British Asians love corn on the cob, roasted under a hot grill and then treated to a generous blob of melting butter before you sink your teeth into the soft kernels. This version uses cut up pieces of corn cob which are given a vivacious splash of Cuban flavour with lime, sugar and chilli along with an Indian touch of *garam masala*.

These will go down well, served up with ice-cold fizzy pop, with young children, hot and hungry from their annual school sports day. Not that I ever participated in sports day. Well, only once. My first attempt was in primary school, where after rapidly realising that I couldn't jump, throw, catch, sprint or do pretty much anything else, I was relegated to the 500 m long distance run. I'll never forget my parents' expressions of pity as the other kids shot away, leaving me panting and clutching the stitch in my side, having barely left the starting line. In fact, the teachers even sent some of the other kids, long finished, to come and help me along, so close was I to collapsing. My Mum quite willingly wrote notes to excuse me from this summer ordeal in years to come, after witnessing my sorry display.

They find it shocking that I am so active now as an adult, practising martial arts and all sorts. I guess there are some things that you grow out of, but I'll never grow out of my love for corn on the cob!

Makes 6 pieces

Method

1 Toss all the ingredients together in a large bowl, making sure the corn cobettes are well coated. Marinate in the fridge for 4 hours.

2 Place the cobettes on a hot grill rack and pour the juices over the top. Grill, turning, until golden brown.

2 corn cobs, each cut into 3 pieces (score well with a sharp knife and then snap apart)

⅓ cup mild olive oil (not virgin or extra virgin)

juice of 1 lime

¼ teaspoon salt

¼ teaspoon garam masala

1 green chilli, finely chopped

1 teaspoon sugar

Fruit, vermicelli and ice cream sundae
Falooda

The year was 1994 and it was the best summer of my life. Not only had I thankfully achieved high grades in my GCSEs, I also had a coveted summer job at the new local Sainsbury's superstore and so for the first time had the financial freedom to buy what in hindsight were the most hideous fashions known to man. I had bought my first pair of contact lenses, which were aqua-coloured (seemed a good idea at the time) and so no longer felt like a frog peering through huge jam-jar circles of glass, and my cousin Nina Bhenji got married in what was a perfect, beautiful, elegant, and rather magical, ceremony.

Indian weddings do not take days, they take weeks. They require years of planning and preparation (indeed some mothers are known to start buying and accumulating items for their daughters' weddings while they are still children) and every day in the week or so in the lead up to the ceremony has its own unique traditions and rituals. Sticky turmeric paste is smeared all over the bride and groom by their respective families, often while they are sitting on a stool in their parents' gardens, wearing their tattiest clothes. The idea is to enhance their complexions before the big day. The bride's maternal uncles dip her bridal bracelets into milk and fit them upon her wrists, performing their last act of protection over her. *Mendhi* (henna) is painted on the bride and young girls while female relatives beat drums with the backs of spoons and dance the thumping *giddha* in the centre of the room.

Much time was spent dancing the evening away in our stunning outfits to the *Mohra* soundtrack in the garden marquee or singing 'Love Is All Around' by Wet, Wet, Wet in honour of the summer's much loved box-office hit, *Four Weddings and a Funeral* while hard-working female relatives cooked utterly delicious, and fresh, food by hand in vat-sized saucepans all day in the garage that was turned into an industrial kitchen. During one of the days, and by popular request from the younger kids who were sick of eating *roti*, they even served freshly cooked chips and beans complete with vinegar and ketchup for the scores of attendees. As I was 16 and therefore just about still considered one of the kids, I got away with more eating and less toiling.

However, my favourite culinary memory of the wedding is that of enjoying this bright pink, ice-cold *falooda* under the summer sun, as made by Nina Bhenji's London *chachiji*. It is like a cross between a milkshake and a sundae, a bit like a knickerbocker glory, made with ice cream, rose syrup, fruit, milk, thin noodle strands and nuts, and is utterly addictive. Thought to have originated in Persia, it was a favourite of Indian Mughal Emperor Jahangir. It is served in a tall milkshake or sundae glass with a long-handled spoon and a straw. You first drink all the milky sweetness with the straw until left with the solid ingredients, which you then scoop up with the spoon. *Serves 4*

Method

small can of fruit cocktail or
    chopped fruit of your choice

1 ball of dried vermicelli, boiled
    until soft (a few minutes) and
    then rinsed and drained with
    cold water

10 g (¼ oz) china grass, broken
    into long strands, boiled for
    2–3 minutes and then rinsed
    and drained with cold water

½ teaspoon tukmaria seeds,
    soaked in a little boiling water
    for 1 hour

4 tablespoons rose syrup

milk

4 large scoops of ice cream

large handful of chopped
    pistachios

1. Take four large, tall milkshake glasses and place a couple of spoonfuls of fruit at the bottom of each.
2. Divide the vermicelli and china grass by four and add to each.
3. Add ½ teaspoon of swollen *tukmaria* seeds to each.
4. Pour in a tablespoon of rose syrup to each glass.
5. Top each glass with milk and stir well.
6. Add a scoop of ice cream and sprinkle with pistachios.
7. Serve with a tall spoon and a straw.

Sweet batter coils
Jalebia

These wispy, sweet, sticky, syrupy, crispy, orange batter coils always
remind me of Indian weddings throughout the summer, indeed it has now
even become the fashion to have your own *jalebi*-maker at weddings,
often in the garden along with the marquee. I was very lucky to be taught
how to make these by the famous Southall Broadway *jalebi*-maker who
stands there day after day at his stall making hot, fresh, mouthwatering
jalebia, in the gigantic boiling oil pan, for hungry, wide-eyed customers.

I used to find the summer wedding season hugely eventful as a
child. We would be treated to several new brightly coloured embroidered
outfits, with matching earrings, necklace, bracelets and packets full of
jewelled *bindia*. However, as a teenager, these outfits caused much
distress, as there would be fights in the car as to who would be the one
to go into the local Sainsbury's after setting off on our journey for that
inevitable one thing we had forgotten to buy. As teenagers who usually
went to great lengths to appear streetwise in trainers, baggy jeans and
hooded tops, we would often have to dash, red-faced and head down, into
the store in all our floaty Indian finery, only to crash straight into some
rather amused kid from school who would no doubt have told the rest of
the class by the new term.

Then there would be the endless car journey on the motorway to
somewhere that seemed to be on the other side of the world in terms of
distance, but when we got there looked no different to where we had
come from, like Bradford, Leeds or Coventry. We would emerge from the
car much less resplendent, all bleary eyed and uncomfortable in, by then,
crumpled clothes. We would often stay over at some hospitable distant
relative's house, huddled on the floor in gigantic, heavy floral Indian
duvets, to be woken up while it was still dark to get ready in time for the
early morning ceremony. I used to hate that part when very young, and
would suffer terrible nausea from it, especially when offered Victoria
sponge cake for my breakfast while trying to fend off my Mum who
was trying to daub me behind the ear with black kohl to ward away the
evil eye.

I would sit in awe, captivated by the streams of older girls and
women entering the *gurudwara* in their stunning outfits, wishing I could be
even a fraction as stylish as them when I grew up, at the same time trying

to keep my *chunni* on my head and avoiding being sat on by some elderly lady. This actually happened to my sister once who was sitting cross-legged, and then suddenly had one leg completely trapped under a rather large, totally unaware, hobbling old stranger who crashed down upon her and then decided not to budge, preferring to continue gossiping and match-making with the purse-lipped lady next to her, rather than paying attention to the marital prayers being recited, only pausing briefly to ask some small child to go and collect extra *Karah Prasad* for her.

The parties afterwards in a local community centre or hall were always great fun with plenty of *samose*, *tandoori* chicken, *jalebia* and *barfi* to be enjoyed before we were hauled on to the dancefloor to demurely jig along to the latest *bhangra* hits being pumped out by the DJ. More often than not, there were also additional spontaneous performances by some *uncleji* who would find a space in the middle of the dancefloor to do a heartfelt song and dance routine around a whisky bottle he had recently become acquainted with and Bacardi-induced men would often hoist each other up on their shoulders, while anxious *auntyjis* would try to stop them from crashing into and squashing the tiered wedding cake.

Have a go with these *jalebia* – it does take practice to perfect the required momentum, timing and pressure, but are so much fun, and delicious, that you will certainly enjoy the process! *Makes 16*

Method

1 Mix the flour and baking powder in a large bowl and then add the food colouring. Mix with enough warm water until you have the consistency of a smooth batter. Cover with cling film and leave to ferment, preferably in an airing cupboard, for 1 hour.

2 Mix the batter with a fork and carefully pour into a large plastic food bag.

3 Place the sugar and water for the syrup in a pan and bring to the boil, stirring to dissolve the sugar, and then turn down to a very low heat – so the heat is just barely on. The syrup is ready when it is of one-thread consistency between your thumb and forefinger. Stir in the food colouring.

4 Keeping a bowl ready to place the bag into, pierce the bag and squeeze about six spirals into oil heated to 170°C to deep-fry. Fry for a few minutes until they are golden and have risen to the top. Remove with a perforated spoon and immerse in the syrup for 30 seconds and then place on a rack. Repeat with all the batter and either serve hot or chilled.

1 cup plain flour
¼ teaspoon baking powder
few drops of yellow food
    colouring

For the syrup
2 cups white granulated sugar
3 cups cold water
few drops of yellow or orange
    food colouring

Gujarati savoury sponge
Dhokla

This cheery yellow Gujarati speciality snack is a gingery, yogurt-fermented *gram* flour savoury sponge, topped with fried mustard seeds and curry leaves. It is eaten during many celebrations, one of them being the traditional August occasion of Rakshabandhan.

Any female friend I have ever explained Rakshabandhan to very quickly goes off and adopts the celebration too. Hindu and Sikh girls buy *rakhria* (decorative, friendship band-style pieces of multicoloured, gold and silver roped thread from Indian shops, only costing from 20p to a £1 each). They then tie one of these on their brother's wrist, symbolic of a charm to keep him protected from harm. In return, the brother promises to act as her protector and gives her money and presents. *Raksha* means protect and *bandhan* means to tie. When I explained that *rakhria* are also tied on dads', uncles' and cousins' wrists, my friends saw pound signs and made their way to the nearest Indian shop to stock up for their newly adopted cash-friendly and female-favoured occasion. The funniest memory I have of Rakshabandhan is from when I was about five years old and we went to Nottingham so that my Mum could tie *rakhria* on her brothers' wrists, the youngest of whom, David Mamma (real name Gurdev), was only 12 or so. My Dad thought to film this on a home video, which led to a very elaborate re-enaction of a Rakshabandan-themed song from an Indian film, beginning with tying the *rakhria* on David Mamma (who was trying desperately to keep a straight face) while my Mum was miming to the song being played in the house, and somehow we all ended up in Wollaton Park with my Mum miming in the park in a sari to a full-blast portable cassette player. My Mum spent most of the time subtly trying to keep David Mamma from running away, who finally resorted to throwing flower heads at my Mum – she happily incorporated this into the song-and-dance routine, with me popping up in the background doing my own little twirls in a pink dress. Watching it makes me have fits of laughter every time, especially when you notice the shocked expressions on the on-looking non-Asian's faces who only came out to walk the dog and seemed to have stumbled straight on to some sort of surreal Indian film set. I hope you celebrate Rakshabandan this year too, and treat your family to these delicious sponges – singing and dancing around parks is strictly optional. *Makes 2 trays – 16 squares per tray*

Method

1 Place the coarse semolina, natural yogurt, *gram* flour and the 3 tablespoons oil together in a large bowl and mix well. Add the warm water and mix thoroughly again until it is the consistency of a cake mix. Cover with cling film and place in an airing cupboard or leave at room temperature overnight.

2 The next day, add the ginger, green chillies, salt, *garam masala* and turmeric and stir.

3 Pour 2 cups of water into a wok that has a lid. Bring to the boil and then turn down to a low heat. Place a steaming rack inside the wok, so that it is not touching the water. Place a 20-cm (8-inch) oiled non-stick cake tin on top of the rack and gently warm.

4 In the meantime, pour 350 ml (12 fl oz) of mixture into a measuring jug and add 1 teaspoon of bicarbonate of soda and stir vigorously with a spoon clockwise.

5 Pour immediately into the warmed tin and cover the wok with the lid immediately to seal.

6 Turn up the heat to high and steam for 15 minutes. Remove the tin and allow to cool before cutting into 16 squares.

7 Place another 2 cups of water in the wok and repeat with the second batch of mixture.

8 Heat the oil in a frying pan and fry the mustard seeds, curry leaves and salt until the mustard seeds begin to splutter and pop.

9 Pour evenly over the *dhokla* squares and serve hot or refrigerate.

2 cups coarse semolina

225 g (8 oz) natural yogurt

¾ cup gram flour

3 tablespoons vegetable oil

1 cup + ½ cup + 3 tablespoons warm water

1 teaspoon grated fresh ginger

1 teaspoon finely chopped green chillies

2 teaspoons salt

1 teaspoon garam masala

¼ teaspoon ground turmeric

2 teaspoons bicarbonate of soda

2 tablespoons oil

4 teaspoons mustard seeds

4 curry leaves

pinch of salt

Bangladeshi fish chop
Sumi's mas bura

In my quest to seek out authentic Bengali cuisine, I decided to take a trip to Brick Lane in London. Starting off at the Whitechapel end, I dodged the gangs of spindly youths in their tight jeans and Ben Sherman shirts, kicking at rubbish on the streets, their gelled hair motionless in the breeze. I was nearly run over by a supermarket trolley stacked high with animal carcasses. I was distracted by the vibrant music stores, blaring out songs from the soundtrack of the latest Indian movie, and wedding shops selling garlands of artificial marigold blossoms.

I then came across a spate of curry houses, one with a picture of Posh and Becks look-alikes eating a meal proudly displayed in the window, with waiters in the doorway luring hungry and willing customers in for a chicken *tikka masala* for lunch. Hungry though I was too, I continued. A few doors further down, I finally saw a few restaurants all proclaiming that they sold the authentic, traditional, real food that British Asians of Bangladeshi origin eat at home. These restaurants certainly looked the real McCoy; they had flung off the shackles of gold and neon signs, pink tablecloths and twangy sitar music: images that had defined the first Indian restaurants in the UK and then, subsequently, the community. Instead, these restaurants had names that celebrated their Sylheti heritage, had stripped wooden floors and were adorned with abstract art. Fantastic, I thought, as I peered towards the window of the first one along my path to check out the menu. By the window of the fifth restaurant, I was considerably depressed. Despite the outward metamorphosis, the menus remained exactly the same.

One restaurant was the most beautiful and promising, so I decided to step inside and find out more. I was welcomed and led to a table where I was presented with a bound menu, the first two pages of which proclaimed that this was a uniquely authentic Bangladeshi restaurant. It was with dismay, therefore, that I turned the pages to again find nothing more than the usual curry house fare. I asked to speak to the head waiter. 'So, all the food served here, and on this menu, is entirely traditional to and originating from Bangladesh?' 'Yes, 100% Bangladeshi speciality,' he replied. 'Are you sure?' I persisted, 'Even the *jalfrezis* and the *tandoori* chicken here?' The extremely loyal waiter went on to elaborate in great detail how all the dishes were indeed authentic. I tentatively ventured, 'But I'm Punjabi, and I know for a fact that *tandoori* chicken originates from the Punjab, and none of these dishes seem to be Bangladeshi to me. I'm a bit confused.'

All the barriers came down as the waiter sat down and finally admitted, 'Okay, so none of the dishes on the menu are from Bangladesh but it is what customers want – they won't accept our real food.' He explained that he believes people want the illusion of authenticity, the funky, trendy image and the fusion beats playing in the background, but are not ready to accept food that strays from what they are used to, such as hotter, unusual tasting dishes, meat with bones and fish with the heads still attached. I felt admiration for these restaurants for adapting to ensure survival.

A few more doors down, I came across a café called Salique's. The window display of this quaint eaterie was a fascinating array of dishes and snacks I had never seen before. Under the name, hung a sign proclaiming it to be real Bangladeshi food, and this time, it seemed to be true. Mr Salique and his colleagues were real characters and Brick Lane stalwarts. They were extremely hospitable and spent time explaining the various dishes to me – which cater for the Bangladeshi residents rather than non-Asian customers – including plenty of hot and dry fish dishes, while filling me in on their social situation. They resented the trendy status the area had recently acquired as this meant that rent was fast increasing, rent they pay to their Jewish landlords who have progressed from the area to North London. The more well-off non-Asians move into the area, the more they have no choice but to move out. The younger generation may want to get out of the ghetto, but they do not want to be forced out. They view the regeneration project not as a mark of respect for their culture, but a patronising form of economic ethnic cleansing. For them, the threat of non-Asian enterprise is fast creeping up on them from the other end of Brick Lane. This part of Brick Lane, the beginning of which is marked by the Old Truman Brewery, is very different. It is full of quirky second-hand and designer clothes shops, offbeat art galleries and unusual cafés populated by artsy media folk sporting asymmetrical hairstyles and 1980s-style plastic earrings and leggings, all of which thrive in this sharp, urban area with its splattering of ethnic credibility. They were also fierce about what they see as snobbery towards them by other British Asians.

'They think they're so much better than us, that we are just common waiters. But we are very proud of who we are and what we have achieved. We were not brought here as servants by the colonial English people. We jumped ship, came here independently and started from scratch, working for ourselves. And we are very proud of our culture – we have a rich heritage in the arts and literature.'

My visit came to a close with Sumi, a sweet natured lady with an even sweeter smile, showing me how to make the following recipe. These Bangladeshi fishcakes in an egg batter can be made with almost any fish, but she suggested tuna. They are very simple to make and are great eaten as a snack with some chutney. *Makes 4*

Method

2 potatoes, peeled, diced, boiled and drained

1 can of tuna (185 g)

handful of chopped coriander

½ teaspoon dried red chilli flakes

½ teaspoon salt

½ teaspoon cumin powder

pinch of ground turmeric

2 eggs, beaten

1 Place all the ingredients, except the eggs, in a bowl and mix well with a fork, gently mashing the potatoes.

2 Shape into four balls and dip each in the bowl of beaten egg to coat thoroughly and then deep-fry immediately until golden brown – about 4 minutes.

Mini mint parathe

These are the cutest little things and are perfect for an intimate dinner party. Tiny balls of *gram* and wheat flour dough, jazzed up with fresh chopped mint leaves, are rolled out into little rounds and then lightly fried in butter on a *thawa* until slightly charred and puffed up. They are a fantastic accompaniment to meat dishes such as Multicolured Pepper Lamb (page 136) but generally go very well with everything. They can even be enjoyed on their own with *dahi* or as part of a *mezze* with a block of feta spiced with red chilli and coriander powder, some *hummous*, a handful of black olives and a dollop of *tzaziki*. *Makes 12*

Method

1 Place the *roti* flour, *gram* flour, salt and mint in a large shallow bowl and mix in enough water, little by little, to be able to knead a firm, smooth dough. Refrigerate for 30 minutes.

2 Heat up the *thawa* on a low heat.

3 Divide the dough into 12 portions and roll each into a small round, dipping into a little extra *roti* flour so that they don't stick.

4 Place three at a time on to the *thawa* and flip over after 10 seconds. Smear them with butter and flip over. Smear the other sides too.

5 Continue to cook, flipping over occasionally, until golden and crispy.

6 Drain on kitchen paper and repeat until all 12 are cooked.

**2 cups roti flour, plus extra for
  rolling
1 cup gram flour
2 teaspoons salt
large handful of chopped mint
butter**

Hot fruit chaat

Chaats, of several varieties, are served on street stalls in India. This vibrant version served hot and made with fresh fruit, or 'fruit fraat' as my Dad says, sizzling straight from the pan is spiced with chilli and soothed with honey and makes for an unusual and refreshing after-dinner dessert.

My friends from Bombay, who now live and work in Britain, love my version of the *chaat* but admit they find British Asians distinctly bizarre and living in some kind of time warp. This is because when the great influx of Indian immigrants arrived in the UK during the 1960s, they brought with them strong cultural and social values, which were very much the order of the day in India at that time.

However, while they have retained these values largely unchanged in their insular communities, India has continued in its logical social and cultural progression. Therefore, while British Asians are proud of the way they have retained their cultural identity, Indians, who are now very modern and liberal, find their ways very old -fashioned and restrictive. For example, a British-Asian girl today wearing her hair in two plaits would be immediately regarded as a sensible and good girl. This becomes interesting when you discover that wearing your hair in two plaits was considered the height of fashion in India in the 1960s and had no connotations of being sensible but rather of having good style, which was itself copied from the West. It is amazing how such simple visual symbols, like plaits, have such interpretive, nostalgic power. *Serves 1–2*

Method

4 strawberries

½ mango, peeled

½ banana, peeled

½ papaya, peeled and deseeded

2 pineapple rings

small handful of pomegranate kernels

few sprigs of coriander, finely chopped

sprinkle of salt

sprinkle of garam masala

sprinkle of red chilli powder

drizzle of honey

1 Dice all the fruit, excluding the pomegranate kernels.

2 Place the fruit in a non-stick frying pan and stir-fry on a medium heat for about 1 minute.

3 Add the coriander, salt, *garam masala* and chilli and give a final stir before spooning it into a serving bowl.

4 Serve with a drizzle of honey on top and with ice cream if you wish.

Coconut chutney

This is a very popular South Indian chutney, eaten with many main dishes such as *idli* and *masala dosa*. Desiccated coconut, popped mustard seeds, garlic, ginger, chilli and coriander are stirred into yogurt, to create an accompaniment that gives your meal a touch of vitality. I thought it would actually be quite difficult to make, but this couldn't be simpler. It is very summery and is great with *parathe*, or with grilled meats or fish with some salad, or as a mixture to include in cold meat sandwiches or baguettes. *Serves 2–6*

Method

1 Pour a drizzle of oil in a pan with the mustard seeds. Fry on a very low heat until they begin to pop and then take the pan immediately off the heat. Be careful with this as you don't want them spitting in your face.

2 Mix the rest of the ingredients together in a bowl using a fork.

3 Add the mustard seeds and mix well.

4 Chill until ready to serve.

drizzle of oil

1 teaspoon mustard seeds

1 cup medium desiccated coconut

8 tablespoons natural low-fat set
   yogurt

1 clove garlic, crushed

1 teaspoon grated fresh ginger

½ small green chilli, finely
   chopped

small handful of finely chopped
   coriander

¼ teaspoon salt

¼ teaspoon garam masala

squeeze of lime

Paneer skewers

I made these for my Dad's 50th birthday party last summer and they look and taste very impressive considering how little time they take to prepare and cook. One word of warning though, eat these as soon as they are cooked because, if you try to reheat them under the grill, the vegetables harden and shrivel up. I was quite adamant about taking care of everything myself, thinking I had the food completely under control while my sister picked out party music and hung up balloons and banners from the ceilings with pictures of our Dad as a child and teenager. Unfortunately, with trays and trays of food being reheated in the one oven, to get everything hot in time for the guests' arrival at the party, it was a typical case of dishes going cold while others were being heated, leading to much reheating and my learning two very important lessons: a) don't reheat food for too long and b) don't try to recreate a restaurant in your Mum's kitchen. However, shrivelly kebabs aside, everyone had a great time, especially my Dad who, like most dads, very rarely gets to be made a fuss of. I'll just have to be more organised for his 60th! *Makes 8 skewers*

Method

8 wooden skewers

600 g (1 lb 5 oz) paneer, cut into chunks

1 red onion, cut into large chunks

2 different coloured peppers, cut into chunks

⅓ cup mild olive oil

1 garlic clove, crushed

1 teaspoon grated fresh ginger

1 teaspoon salt

1 teaspoon garam masala

1 teaspoon dried red chilli flakes

2 teaspoons coriander powder

1 tablespoon lemon juice

handful of chopped coriander

1 Soak the skewers in water for 30 minutes to prevent them burning.

2 Combine all the ingredients together in a large bowl, cover with cling film and refrigerate for 30 minutes.

3 Tightly thread on to the skewers and grill on a high heat for about 8–10 minutes, turning every few minutes, until golden.

Indian flag pizza

I bought my Mum a breadmaker for Christmas last year and it has fast become the favourite gadget in the house. My sister's favourite food is pizza so we now regularly make our own fresh pizzas and experiment with toppings. This is one of our favourites with its creamy but salty white feta cheese, roasted deep orange butternut squash and emerald green baby spinach resembling the colours of the Indian flag, created in honour of the anniversary of India's independence in August 1947.

I regard this anniversary as a rather bittersweet occasion. It is unquestionably a time to celebrate India's independence of colonial domination. However, it is also a time for reflection. Most Indians, within India and across the diaspora, know, and have always known, that if it were not for the preoccupations of factional in-fighting, it is unlikely that the British Raj, through the East India trade company, would have gained its foothold within India, allowing them to take the first step of colonisation and eventually trampling over all of India. Yet despite this knowledge, few lessons have been learnt.

Since Independence there has been Partition, bloodshed and continuous violent fragmentation in the name of religion. Gandhi's message has been disregarded at every opportunity. Most English people are aware of Hindu Muslim division but are unaware that the root of this division lies in more than religious differences. Prior to Partition, most villages contained a proportion of both Hindus and Muslims, and Sikhs too. Of course, Indian history is studded with clashes between these groups but, on the whole, they lived in harmony, predominantly respectful of each other's religious beliefs and cultural practices. However, amidst the fever of Partition, many violent atrocities were committed against each other that left deep, bitter wounds. It is largely due to the painful memories of these experiences that such divisions exist today.

The caste system, which Gandhi opposed, is also still very much alive today for British Asians. This system refers to what jobs families traditionally did back in India, such as carpentry or goldsmiths. However, although respected as a way of maintaining traditional ties and identity, Sikhs do not believe in the caste system as a form of hierarchy. It is also becoming confusing with the social mobility available to the British-Asian second and third generations through education. Maybe there will be a new system with Doctor, Lawyer, IT, Estate Agent, and Media castes!

Who knows? But in the meantime, enjoy this crispy pizza with its exquisite combination of flavours, set off by a smattering of pomegranate kernels – the real jewels of India. *Serves 2–4*

Method

1 Drizzle the butternut squash with olive oil and bake in an oven preheated to 230°C, Gas Mark 8 for 20 minutes.

2 Whizz the tomatoes, garlic, red chilli flakes, *garam masala* and salt in a blender until smooth. Spread this over the base using the back of a spoon.

3 Top evenly with the mozzarella and onion.

4 Cover evenly with the spinach and then sprinkle over the feta and butternut squash. Season with salt and pepper and drizzle with olive oil.

5 Bake in the oven for 30 minutes.

6 Sprinkle with the pomegranate kernels, if desired, and slice.

large pizza base, preferably home-made

¼ butternut squash, diced

½ cup tinned chopped tomatoes

2 cloves of garlic

½ teaspoon dried red chilli flakes

½ teaspoon garam masala

good pinch of salt

125 g (4½ oz) mozzarella cheese, cut into cubes

¼ red onion, sliced thinly

2 handfuls of torn baby spinach leaves

100 g (3½ oz) feta cheese, cut into cubes

salt and coarsely ground pepper, to season

drizzle of olive oil

small handful of pomegranate kernels (optional)

Finely diced relish
Kachumbar

You may recognise this as the finely chopped salad often served with poppadoms in Indian restaurants. Fresh green chilli, used deseeded here so as not to set your mouth on fire, gives the onion, tomato and cucumber mixture bite and it is also lifted with a splash of lemon. Serve this colourful combination as an accompaniment with any of your main meals or use it to fill tortilla wraps or as a burger relish. *Serves 4*

Method

4 tomatoes, deseeded and very finely chopped

½ cucumber, very finely chopped

1 onion, very finely chopped

1 green chilli, deseeded and very finely chopped

splash of lemon juice

coriander sprigs

Simply mix all the ingredients, apart from the coriander, together in a bowl and then garnish with the sprigs of coriander.

Sparkling rose syrup water
Rooh afza

This is such a pretty summer drink, with its floral bouquet, and is capable of quenching any thirst. Deep magenta, full-bodied, rose syrup is poured over a cluster of glinting ice cubes and topped with a sparkling cascade of chilled spring or mineral water. *Rooh afza* is used all over India and is also a common Middle Eastern ingredient but here it is used to concoct a refresher that will impress at any gathering. Try serving it in a large glass jug topped with freshly picked rose petals. *Serves 1*

Method

1 Place the ice at the bottom of a tall glass.

2 Pour in the rose syrup – half the amount you would add when using cordial or squash, as it is very strong.

3 Top with sparkling water.

ice cubes

rose syrup

sparkling water

In the distance, fireflies spit and crackle,

Their incandescence licking above the cremated logs,

Reflected in the coruscation of the eyes of rosy cheeked spectators,

Brandishing wands of sparkles like frenzied sorcerers,

Wild Catherine wheels reeling out of control,

Missiles of Technicolor dynamite rocket into the blank sky,

Whilst a pathway of devout diva lamps of clay light the way home for Rama and Sita...

AUTUMN

Balti lamb

Baltis are particularly loved in Birmingham, where there is a profusion of *balti* restaurants. There are many theories as to where the name *balti* comes from. One is that the style of cooking originates from a place called Baltistan near Pakistan. Others claim that *balti* dishes are the same as *karahi* dishes but they were given the name *balti* as the British couldn't pronounce *karahi*. I was in my teens when the *balti* first became popular, and it was certainly the first time I had heard of this style of cooking. I remember being utterly confused as, in Punjabi, *balti* means bucket. In fact, in our house, the word was synonymous with a certain blue plastic bucket brought out whenever we were ill as children as a form of sick bucket. Once I tasted certain *balti* dishes, however, they were delicious enough to distract me from this visual image.

This hot lamb variety uses a very important method used by some restaurants to precook the meat in boiling water until it is unbelievably soft, freed of fat and infused with garlic and ginger. It is then quickly stir-fried. When I cooked it with ginger, tomatoes, chilli, coriander powder, cumin powder, black pepper and butter, my Dad exclaimed this was better than any other version he had tried. *Serves 4*

Method

1 Place the lamb in a pan with 3 cups of water, the garlic, ginger and salt and stir well. Bring to the boil, cover and simmer on a low heat for 1 hour.

2 In a large frying pan, wok or *karahi*, heat the oil and add the ginger and garlic. Stirring continuously, fry until golden brown.

3 Add the tomatoes and stir-fry until they are well blended into the garlic and ginger and the oil separates out.

4 Gently remove the garlic cloves from the pan with the lamb, and then drain the lamb. Add the lamb to the tomato mixture and stir-fry with the chilli, salt, coriander powder, cumin powder, red chilli powder and ½ cup of water.

5 Add the onion and halved chillies and keep stir-frying on a medium to high heat until you have a small amount of rich, thick sauce – about 5–7 minutes.

6 Switch off the heat, stir in the butter and sprinkle with the coriander.

To prepare the lamb

650 g (1 lb 7½ oz) cubed lamb

6 cloves garlic, peeled

1 tablespoon grated fresh ginger

sprinkle of salt

For the sauce

½ cup oil

1 tablespoon grated fresh ginger

1 tablespoon crushed garlic

3 fresh tomatoes, chopped

4 green chillies, finely chopped

1 teaspoon salt

3 teaspoons coriander powder

3 teaspoons cumin powder

1 teaspoon red chilli powder

½ teaspoon black pepper

½ onion, finely sliced

2 green chillies, cut in half lengthways but not de-seeded

1 tablespoon butter

handful of chopped coriander

Black pepper and double coriander lamb

This is a rich, intense dish of meltingly soft cubes of lamb in a dense, dark green, coriander sauce. The sauce is made by cooking bunches of freshly chopped coriander leaves until they are broken down into a blanket of forest green, spiced with the woody scent of black pepper, cloves and coriander seeds. This is just the thing on a darkening autumn evening, but, as the sauce is so powerful, I recommend only allowing yourself a small portion – if you can. It is delicious with buttery *naan* and cumin *raita*, but I prefer stirring it into a portion into plain basmati rice and eating it with a dollop of *dahi*. *Serves 4*

Method

1 Place the lamb in a hot, dry, non-stick pan or wok and stir with a wooden spoon, on a medium heat, browning all over for about 5 minutes. Drain the fat away and place the meat aside.

2 Heat the oil in a large pan and add the onion, garlic, peppercorns and cloves.

3 When the onions are a deep golden brown, take the pan off the heat for a few seconds and add the tomatoes. Stir well and turn the heat to low.

4 Add the chillies, ginger, turmeric, *garam masala*, salt and a splash of water.

5 Stirring occasionally, when the mixture becomes shiny and the oil separates, add the chopped coriander. Turn the heat up to medium and stir well to mix.

6 Add the lamb, stirring thoroughly to coat. Add 2½ cups of boiling water, stir well, bring to the boil and then reduce to a simmer. Cover and cook on a low heat for 25 minutes.

7 Stir well, turn up the heat to medium and reduce to a thick sauce, stirring occasionally, for 10 minutes.

8 Stir in the ground coriander and remove from the heat.

9 Garnish with fresh coriander.

800 g (1 lb 12 oz) cubed boneless lamb, washed

¼ cup of oil

1 large onion, finely chopped

3 cloves garlic, finely chopped

1 teaspoon black peppercorns

3 cloves

½ cup canned chopped tomatoes

2 green chillies, finely chopped

1 tablespoon grated fresh ginger

1 teaspoon ground turmeric

2 teaspoons garam masala

1½ teaspoon salt

2 bunches (80 g/2¾ oz each) fresh coriander, finely chopped

1 teaspoon ground coriander

coriander leaves, to garnish

Deep-fried crispy chicken balls with tangy tomato sauce

These were inspired by a Hong Kong style sweet-and-sour chicken Chinese takeaway dish that my sister and I absolutely love. It is minced chicken in a crispy batter served with a thick, orange sauce. My Dad always thought it might be an idea to try to create a similar dish with Indian flavours. I decided upon a chicken mince combined with ginger, coriander powder, cumin powder and lemon. My sister was intrigued and even pitched in with making them, perfecting a technique for rolling the balls in flour. She also perfected a technique for gobbling them down straight from the fryer and I nearly didn't have enough left to serve with the sauce. The sauce is a tomato-based sweet-and-sour sauce, with *tandoori masala*, chilli and sugar, that is best drizzled over them. So next time you feel like cosying in on a cold evening, give these a try instead of your usual takeaway. *Serves 4–6*

Method

1 Place the chicken mince, onion, ginger, green chillies, garlic, lemon juice, salt, *garam masala*, cumin powder and coriander powder in a large bowl and mix well with a fork. Add the egg and continue to mix thoroughly.

2 Cover with cling film and refrigerate for 30 minutes.

3 In the meantime, heat the oil in a pan and add the crushed garlic and ginger. Fry, stirring continuously, until golden brown.

4 Remove the pan from the heat for a few seconds and then add the tomatoes, *tandoori masala*, salt, turmeric, chilli and sugar. Stir well and turn the heat to low.

5 When the mixture is shiny and the oil has separated out, add the coriander and ½ cup water and stir until you have a well blended, even sauce. Leave to cool.

6 Place the self-raising flour in a large bowl and add enough water to make a smooth, thick batter.

7 Roll the chicken mixture into 22 balls and then roll each one in self-raising flour to coat. Dip in the batter and deep-fry in batches of about five in oil heated to 180°C for 10 minutes. Drain on kitchen paper.

8 When all the chicken balls are fried, heat up the sauce in the pan and pour over the chicken balls or use as a dip.

500 g (1 lb 2 oz) chicken mince

½ onion, grated and squeezed of all juice

1 tablespoon grated fresh ginger

4 green chillies, finely chopped

2 cloves garlic, crushed

good splash of lemon juice

1½ teaspoons salt

2 teaspoons garam masala

½ teaspoon cumin powder

½ teaspoon coriander powder

1 egg, beaten

For the sauce

4 tablespoons oil

1 teaspoon crushed garlic

1 teaspoon grated fresh ginger

½ cup canned chopped tomatoes

½ teaspoon tandoori masala

½ teaspoon salt

½ teaspoon powder turmeric

1½ green chillies, finely chopped

½ teaspoon sugar

handful of chopped coriander

For the batter

1 cup self-raising flour, plus extra for coating

Cauliflower florets
Gobi di sabji

Autumn is always marked by a celebration of harvest. In India, the Hindu festival of Dassera takes place in early autumn and marks a welcome period of leisure, enjoyment and abundance. The sky is often clear, the air fresh and the weather pleasant and mild. Such gentleness is also carried through into relationships, as a concilliatory atmosphere of peace, goodwill, friendship and sharing is fostered and personal disagreements are buried. In this community spirit, Hindus exchange gifts and sweets with each other, and in Gujarat the women dance the famous *garba* – a fascinatingly precise and vibrant dance with sticks.

Dassera is very similar to the British Harvest Festival tradition, with which I am more familiar. I would love the Harvest Festival each year at school, and enjoyed the practice of delivering food to the elderly in our area. Granted, some opened the door and looked at me rather quizzically as I stood there on their doorstep beaming away, clutching several tins of beans, mushy peas and a marrow (I am sure they thought British Asians didn't eat such things!), but most were friendly to me and very grateful.

There are certain earthy, rustic *sabjia*, which are best enjoyed in the autumn, and this traditional *gobi sabji* is one of them. Some families prefer to keep the florets quite large and also add pieces of potato, but I prefer it like this with small florets and given an extra dimension with the addition of fenugreek leaves. Eat with hearty *parathe* or even mash up the *sabji* and use it to stuff a *paratha*, as commonly done on cold mornings when a more filling breakfast is required. *Serves 4*

Method

1 Heat the butter in a large pan and add the cumin seeds. When sizzling, add the onion and garlic and fry until a light golden brown.

2 Remove the pan from the heat for a few seconds and then add the tomatoes, ginger, chillies, turmeric, salt, *garam masala* and fenugreek leaves. Cook on a low heat until the mixture is shiny and the oil separates out.

3 Add the cauliflower and turn up the heat to medium. Stir-fry, coating the cauliflower thoroughly, for a couple of minutes.

4 Add a ¼ cup of water, stir well, cover and steam through on a very low heat for 15–20 minutes, stirring occasionally, very gently. Sprinkle with the coriander.

2 tablespoons butter

2 teaspoons cumin seeds

1 onion, finely chopped

1 clove garlic, finely chopped

⅓ cup canned chopped tomatoes

1 tablespoon grated fresh ginger

2 green chillies, finely chopped

1 teaspoon powder turmeric

1½ teaspoons salt

1 teaspoon garam masala

handful of fresh fenugreek leaves, finely chopped

1 cauliflower head, cut into small florets, large florets halved or quartered

handful of coriander, finely chopped

Rice and potato saffron mash

As a child, Autumn was always my favourite season. The back-to-school atmosphere filled me with optimism at the beginning of the academic year – seeing my friends again, conker contests in the playground, starting new classes and learning new things that I would never use again, kicking my way through piles of papery fallen leaves with shiny new T-bar shoes, the smell of a fresh new plastic pencil case filled with multicoloured pencils lingering in the air.

Okay, so, yes, I was the kind of geeky kid whose favourite present ever was a set of 100 felt tip pens and who never quite got the point of Barbie dolls, Sylvanian Families and My Little Ponies (though I pester-powered my parents to buy me one of each, as all my friends had them, only to stare at them for an hour before throwing them in the toy box in favour of Spirograph or Etch-a-Sketch – which incidentally, and to my howling dismay, my Mum broke by stepping on it while dancing along to *Top of the Pops*) but almost everyone has nostalgic memories about going back to school in autumn.

I was very lucky in that my Mum didn't work when my brother and I were young, so we were totally spoilt with fresh, home-cooked meals every day and not the convenience food that so many children eat nowadays. Along with the Indian food that created my life-long love affair with it, we were also fed wonderful English dishes such as cheese and potato pie, raisin and brown sugar stuffed baked apples, chicken casserole, roasts and lots of creamy mash and gravy.

Mash is always a winner with hungry school children, but here is a version that is exotic enough for grown-ups too. It goes just as well with sausages as it does with Black Pepper and Double Coriander Lamb (page 103) or baked chicken like Green Masala Chicken Breasts (page 66). Omit the red chilli slices if you are serving it to children. *Serves 2*

Method

good pinch of saffron strands

½ cup warm milk

2 baking potatoes, peeled, chopped
   into small cubes and rinsed,
   then boiled and drained

butter

½ teaspoon salt

½ teaspoon garam masala

sprinkle of lemon juice

¼ cup rice, washed and boiled

1 large red chilli, sliced into
   rounds

1 Soak the saffron in the warm milk for 30 minutes.

2 Place the potatoes in a pan with the saffron milk and a good knob of butter and mash well on a very low heat.

3 Add the salt, *garam masala*, lemon juice and stir. Gently stir in the rice.

4 Mash well with another good knob of butter.

5 Top with the red chilli slices (if using) and serve.

Simple cumin rice *Zeera Chaul*

The autumn that you fly the nest to begin life as a university student is always a momentous one. There you are, settling in, putting up the obligatory Bob Marley or Indian film star poster on the wall, setting your candles on the window sill, lining up your shiny books and folders on the shelf, twining fairy lights around the mirror, stacking your CDs next to the desk lamp. Your stomach rumbles, but there is no *mummyji* around calling you to the table where a hearty meal is sitting waiting for you. The canteen food is so bad you'd rather eat your own hand and the communal kitchen consists of a rusty electric hob that hasn't been used since the 1970s. But before you slide down the slippery slope into pot noodle land or run to catch the next train home, there are many tasty, simple dishes you can quickly make requiring minimal kitchen appliances and utensils.

Rice is always a good bet as it stores well, cooks quickly, is healthy and filling and can be very versatile. Try this simple but very tasty cumin rice, which can be eaten with anything from yogurt to baked beans for a very cheap quick meal that will no doubt impress your fellow students. *Serves 4*

Method

1 tablespoon oil

2 teaspoons cumin seeds

½ onion, thinly sliced

1 teaspoon salt

2 cups basmati rice, washed

1 Heat the oil in a pan and add the cumin seeds. When they begin to sizzle, add the onion and salt. Fry until the onions are softened.

2 Add the rice and stir-fry for 2 minutes.

3 Add 2¾ cups of cold water and bring to the boil.

4 Stir well. Reduce the heat to low, partly cover and simmer for 15–20 minutes, until all the water has evaporated.

5 Loosen gently with a fork and transfer to a serving dish.

Batter drops in syrup *Sweet Bhoondi*

These raindrop-like balls of pink batter soaked in sugar syrup are an indulgent snack to brighten up any gloomy evening. They are made with the same type of batter as *jalebia* but the batter is poured through a perforated spoon into hot oil, which sizzles each drop as it falls into the pan. After being dunked in the sugar syrup, they dry to crispy on the outside and juicy on the inside. Eat immediately or refrigerate and eat cold. You can also make different brightly coloured batches and use them as an ice cream topping.
Serves 2

Method

1 Place the flour and baking powder in a large bowl and mix well with a spoon. Add the food colouring and mix with enough warm water until you have a smooth batter. Cover with cling film and leave to ferment, preferably in an airing cupboard, for 1 hour.

2 Mix well with a fork.

3 Place the sugar and water for the syrup in a pan and bring to the boil, stirring to dissolve the sugar, and then turn down to a very low heat – so the heat is just barely on. The syrup is ready when it is of one thread consistency between your thumb and forefinger. Stir in the food colouring.

4 Holding a perforated spoon above oil heated to 170°C to deep-fry, gently pour the batter through the perforated spoon. You should have lots of little balls floating to the surface.

5 Once they have risen to the surface – a couple of minutes – remove with a clean perforated spoon, drain quickly on kitchen paper and dunk into the syrup for about 20 seconds and remove. Place in a bowl and chill.

½ cup plain flour

pinch of baking powder

few drops of pink food colouring

For the syrup

2 cups (500 g) white granulated sugar

3 cups cold water

few drops of pink food colouring

Date and honey phirni

This creamy ground rice chilled dessert is made with dates, honey and milk and was inspired by my friend Miriam as a dish with which to break fast during the Islamic month of Ramadan, currently held in autumn. Honey, dates and milk are recommended as foods to eat by the prophet Mohammed in the *Qur'an*. Dates in particular are singled out as an appropriate food to break fast with. Ramadan is a quiet, serious and contemplative month when no food or water is consumed between dawn and sunset. Perfume, chewing gum and impure or uncharitable thoughts or behaviour are also abstained from. The majority of time is spent in prayer and meditation as this is the month in which the *Qur'an* was first revealed to the prophet.

In celebration of this occasion, healthy and able Muslims sacrifice the material pleasures of food and water as an offering to God and to express their gratitude. It is believed that the process of fasting, one of the five pillars of Islam, teaches self-discipline and also enables the rich to experience poverty and hunger first hand, not only allowing them to further appreciate how lucky they are to have such abundance in their lives but also to empathise with and do more for the poor. In the current Islamaphobic political climate where Islam seems to equal suicide bombers in many minds, the concept of *jihad* has become synonymous with war. Few people know that *jihad* means personal struggle and that Ramadan is one of the most important expressions of this.

On a secular level, while we in the West are becoming more and more obese, with effortless access to almost any type of food in the world right on our doorsteps and fast food outlets on every corner, we are becoming increasingly disconnected from those who have to walk miles every day just for a few sips of dirty, polluted water. I think it would be an invaluable experience for all of us lucky people in the West to maybe sacrifice the well-documented three McDonald's a day and try to fast for a week to open our eyes to what others around the world endure, and then perhaps we would do more to help them.

I had a very minor experience of this last year in New York. It was the 4th of July and my friend Louise and I had planned to spend the day walking through Central Park and then go straight on to FDR Drive for the famous 4th of July fireworks display over the Hudson River. We ended up wearing the most inappropriate clothing (jeans, T-shirts, socks and trainers) for what turned out to be the hottest and most humid day of the year there so far. By the time we got to the celebrations on the river we were miserably uncomfortable.

In the rush to get a good place to view the fireworks, we didn't stop to buy any refreshments before heading in, thinking there would be provisions inside. However, as we began to notice that every single American was carrying a cool box and several litres of water, we started to panic. The heat was sweltering, our mouths like sandpaper and a sinking feeling entered the pit of our stomachs when we were told that there were no refreshments and that we could not leave to buy any.

With five hours to go, this suddenly felt like hell. There were cops standing patrol, each with a huge crateful of bottles of water. Great, we thought, we will ask if we can buy a bottle from them. No such luck, the 30 bottles per cop were apparently for their personal use only. We were close to fainting and, after having desperately begged the sixth cop only to be flatly refused and threatened with being taken away in an ambulance, surrounded by hundreds of Americans all glugging from their plentiful bottles, I realised how much we take for granted the precious commodity of drinking water. 'Sweaty jeans day' was a definite turning point for me.

When I was honing all the recipes for this book and cooking every day for over a month, I kept a portion from everything I made and took it to the homeless in my area. So when you make and enjoy this luxurious little sweet, take a moment to consider the enlightened concept celebrated this season of empathising with and helping your fellow man, a crucial idea supported by all religions. *Serves 4–6*

Method

1 Place the milk and sugar in a large saucepan on a medium heat.

2 When the sugar has dissolved, stir in the rice powder, and the ground almonds, cashews and pistachios.

3 Bring to the boil, stirring occasionally, as the mixture will begin to thicken.

4 Add the evaporated milk, chopped dates, rose water and ground cardamom.

5 Reduce the heat, stir and simmer for 10 minutes. Stir continuously throughout this time as it will thicken dramatically.

6 Remove from the heat and pour into little serving bowls.

7 Decorate with the whole nuts, sliced dates and drizzle with honey.

8 Refrigerate until ready to serve.

450 ml (16 fl oz) whole milk

75 g (2¾ oz) light brown soft sugar

60 g (2¼ oz) ground rice powder

1 tablespoon ground almonds

1 tablespoon ground cashews

1 tablespoon ground pistachios

500 g tin evaporated milk

50 g (1¾ oz) stoned dates, finely chopped

2 tablespoons rose water

1 teaspoon ground cardamom

handful of whole pistachios and/or cashews

6 whole dates, stoned and sliced into thin strips

1 tablespoon honey

Pumpkin kofte

Halloween was so much more fun when I was younger. There were themed fancy dress activities at school, which I would attend wearing a black bin-liner cloak and a pointy witch's hat with glued-on silver stars, cobwebs scrawled on my face with my Mum's make-up. Although we were never allowed to go trick or treating, there was always plenty of fun to be had at home in those days with programmes like *The Worst Witch*, or pumpkins to carve, and we would get sweet treats and presents like skeleton-topped pens and cackling toy witches; my brother and I would play ghoulish versions of hide and seek around the house. My Dad, like lots of British-Asian fathers, was never completely convinced by the practice of trick or treating, viewing the egg throwing as an act of sheer vandalism, and we would often have to stop him from going out and giving the kids a good old-fashioned hiding.

Interestingly, the Hindu and Sikh festival of Diwali, which almost coincides with Halloween and has many meanings, has elements associated with spirits and the dead, linking it very closely to Halloween. One reason for the lighting of lamps during Diwali is to guide the souls of dead relatives to heaven. Another is to drive away evil from the world in the hope of better times. In West Bengal the occasion is dedicated to worshipping Kali, who rules over death and has skeletons and ghosts as her loyal followers. The lamps are lit to honour her and in return she promises the renewal of life. In Maharashtra it is a festival for warding off the ruler of the underworld, King Bali.

Instead of making pumpkin soup with the leftover flesh from pumpkins that have had lopsided menacing grins hacked into them, try these for a Halloween supper. Kids will love making the little balls of mixture too. These *kofte* are like vegetarian meatballs made from grated pumpkin flesh, mixed with *gram* flour and spices, then deep-fried and stirred at the last minute into a *thari*, soaking and softening them. Eat with *roti* smeared with a little butter. *Serves 4*

Method

1 Place the grated pumpkin, *gram* flour, ginger, chilli, salt and *garam masala* in a large bowl and mix well with a large spoon.

2 Roll the mixture into 20 small balls, a little smaller than golf balls. Do this by gently squeezing and tossing from palm to palm, only squeezing and shaping very lightly as otherwise too much water will be released and the mixture won't hold in the shape of a ball.

3 Place the balls on a plate covered with two sheets of kitchen paper until ready to fry.

4 Deep-fry in batches at 170°C for 8 minutes until golden brown and crispy.

5 Drain on kitchen paper while making the *thari* (sauce).

6 Heat the oil and butter in a large pan and add the onion and garlic. Fry until golden brown.

7 Remove the pan from the heat for a few seconds and add the tomatoes, ginger, chillies, salt, turmeric, *garam masala*, *tandoori masala*, one handful of chopped coriander and ¼ cup of water. Cook on a low heat until the mixture is shiny and the oil separates out.

8 Add a further 2 cups of water and stir well. Bring to the boil and then simmer, partly covered, for 15 minutes. Remove the lid, turn up the heat and thicken for 1–2 minutes. You should have plenty of evenly blended sauce.

9 Add the pumpkin *kofte* and stir very gently once. Cook on a very low heat for a few minutes, just to heat through, and then serve.

450 g (1 lb) grated pumpkin flesh

4 tablespoons gram flour

2 teaspoons grated fresh ginger

1 teaspoon finely chopped green chilli

1 teaspoon salt

1½ teaspoons garam masala

For the thari (sauce)

2 tablespoons oil

1 teaspoon butter

1 onion, finely chopped

1 clove garlic, finely chopped

½ cup canned chopped tomatoes

2 teaspoons grated fresh ginger

2 green chillies, finely chopped

1 teaspoon salt

1 teaspoon turmeric powder

3 teaspoons garam masala

½ teaspoon tandoori masala

2 handfuls of chopped coriander

Mini pickling-spice-stuffed aubergine bake

I'm sure there are many of you who will agree with me when I say that no matter how many years you practise, your cooking never tastes as good as your mother's. This is certainly true for me and I believe it should be no other way. Using the same ingredients and the same techniques, my Mum's food always has the extra something special that I just can't replicate. And she says the same thing of her own Mum's cooking.

My Mum used to make this warming, comforting dish of mini whole aubergines stuffed with an onion *masala* quite a lot when I was little – here with the addition of *panch puran* pickling spices layered with thin veneers of potato and baked until golden. Last year we were busy preparing food for my Dad's 50th birthday party and I was intent on doing most of the cooking myself, industriously churning out fancy snacks and quirky finger food and arranging them on pieces of bright pink and gold tissue. Then literally right at the end my Mum whizzes up this amazing retro dish out of nowhere and needless to say it was the most raved about dish at the party. And despite my Mum being very complimentary about the food I had made, there was just no contest. This is great as a side or main dish with *roti* or *pooria*. And just the thing for a dinner party, served with some creamed or wilted spinach. *Serves 2–4*

Method

6 mini aubergines

3 tablespoons oil

2 teaspoons cumin seeds

½ teaspoon panch puran pickling
  spices

1 onion, finely chopped

½ cup canned chopped tomatoes

1 tablespoon grated fresh ginger

2 green chillies, finely chopped
  with seeds

1½ teaspoons salt

1 teaspoon turmeric powder

1½ teaspoons garam masala

1 teaspoon dried mango powder

handful of chopped coriander

1 potato, peeled, sliced in half
  lengthways and then into thin
  slices widthways

coriander sprigs, to garnish

1 Preheat the oven to 200°C, Gas Mark 6.

2 Holding each aubergine upside down, use a sharp small knife to cut lengthways up to the stalk, but not through. Do this widthways too. What you should have is an aubergine quartered up to but still attached to the stalk.

3 Heat 2 tablespoons of oil in a frying pan and add the aubergines. Fry lightly, turning them over, until soft and slightly golden. Remove from the heat.

4 Heat the remaining oil in a pan and add the cumin seeds and *panch puran*. When sizzling – only a few seconds – remove the pan from the heat and then add the tomato, ginger, chillies, salt, turmeric, *garam masala*, dried mango powder and coriander.

5 Stir on a low heat until the mixture becomes shiny and the oil separates.

6 Using your fingers, gently open the quarters of the aubergine, but being careful to keep it intact, and use a teaspoon to fill each aubergine with the *masala* mixture.

7 Place the aubergines in a casserole dish and cover with a layer of the potatoes. Cover tightly with foil and bake in the over for 1 hour.

8 Garnish with coriander.

Raisin chutney

This is a speedy, coarse chutney packed with autumnal dried fruit ground down with both red and green chillies, ginger, cumin and lime for a mellow and fruity jam-like accompaniment to plain *roti*, bangers and mash, and any savoury deep-fried snacks. Keep it in the fridge for up to 1 week. *Makes a tubful*

Method

1 Place all the ingredients, apart from the coriander, in a grinder and blend until you have a thick coarse paste.
2 Stir in the coriander.

200 g (7 oz) raisins

2 green chillies, chopped

2 red chillies, chopped

1 teaspoon grated fresh ginger

1 teaspoon cumin powder

juice of 2 limes

pinch of salt

1 tablespoon chopped coriander

Fried plantain chips *Mottoke*

These brittle chips of finely sliced plaintain (a firmer, greener, more savoury member of the banana family) are enjoyed in parts of Africa, the Caribbean and the Deep South but are also widely appreciated by British Asians. Ready-fried bags of them are available in Indian grocery shops and in some sweet and snack shops, which is where I first came across them.

I recently enjoyed a trip to Ghana where I was lucky enough to try some of their own recipes for plantain. I was treated to plantain baked in its skin, fried plantain and boiled plantain, all truly delicious. Whilst I was there, I also discovered many similarities between Ghanaian and British Asian culture – they too hand their recipes down by word of mouth from mother to child and, like many British Asians, often have a bottle of chilli sauce to hand at mealtimes to spice up their food! Their cuisine was very similar in terms of flavours to some of our British Asian dishes: Jollof Rice was a particular favourite of mine. In addition, their values, especially those relating to family and education, were so similar to those of British Asian families, that I felt right at home! *Serves 4*

Method

4 mottoke (plantain), about 800 g (1 lb 12 oz)

salt

red chilli powder

1 Peel the *mottoke* and cut at a slight diagonal into thin round slices.
2 Deep-fry in batches at 170°C for 5 minutes.
3 Drain and sprinkle liberally with salt and chilli powder.

Cassava chips *Mogo*

I enjoyed these recently at a 1st birthday party for my cousin Nina Bhenji's little baby daughter, Symriti. A Gujarati speciality, these are made from cassava, a yam-like vegetable. The skin is peeled off with a knife and the opaque white flesh is then cut into chips and deep-fried until lightly golden and crispy on the outside, much the same as with potato chip,s but with a much lower glycaemic index. They are then splashed with lemon juice and sprinkled with salt and chilli powder, just as potato chips are treated to a dash of salt and vinegar. Eat them on their own as a snack or try as a substitute for potato chips with fried eggs and beans. *Serves 2–4*

Method

1 Peel and chop the cassava into chips.

2 Deep-fry in batches at 170°C for 7–8 minutes.

3 Drain and sprinkle with salt, red chilli powder and lemon juice.

1 cassava, about 600 g (1 lb 5 oz)

salt

red chilli powder

lemon juice

Sweet potato jackets with chilli masala butter

One of the highlights of the season of autumn is Bonfire Night, with its showering fireworks setting the night sky ablaze, sparklers dizzily crackling effervescent colour and people wrapped up eating jacket potatoes and burgers around flaming bonfires. We British Asians are very lucky in that we get to do this twice in a fortnight with both Bonfire Night and Diwali.

As children we would stand eagerly in the garden, swirling our sparklers awaiting the display of each magnificent rocket, banger or Catherine wheel as my Dad would go and plant each one in the frosty earth, lighting it with the long wick. We once had a Bonfire Night that was slightly more exciting than we had anticipated when my Dad lit a large bulbous firework and, instead of it shooting upwards as planned, it span out of all control and zoomed around the garden, then made a beeline for us standing, frozen with terror, on the patio in front of the open back door. We all ran for cover inside slamming the door just in time (I ungainly crashed into a washing basket), peeking out at the flashes of green light from the heat-seeking missile in the garden. None of us was hurt, just a little bruised, but we developed a distinct preference for either sparklers only, or organised displays, after that.

Last year we attended a truly magnificent display at a local showground, clutching our food with numb, blue fingers. Jacket potatoes are the perfect food for Bonfire Night, along with sloppy joes. When I was very little we would have dark, crusty, blistered jacket potatoes baked properly in the oven (as opposed to the inferior microwave versions of today) as a post-firework supper, often served with relish. Try these sweet potato jackets, with their fiery-coloured orange flesh, to ring the changes. If you're having a garden barbecue with your bonfire or firework display, wrap them in foil and let them cook away, then mash a tangy portion of chilli, *garam masala*, lemon and coriander butter into the soft flesh when cooked. *Serves 1*

Method

1 sweet potato

butter

sea salt and pepper, to season

squeeze of lemon juice

sprinkle of garam masala

**few sprigs of coriander, finely
    chopped**

**few sprinklings of green chilli,
    finely chopped**

1 Scrub the potato, stab all over, rub with a little butter and season with salt and pepper. Wrap in foil and bake in an oven preheated to 220°C, Gas Mark 7, for 1 hour.

2 Mix a tablespoon of butter with the remaining ingredients and a sprinkle of salt in a bowl with a fork.

3 Unwrap the potato, split with a knife and top with butter mixture.

Besan peanut brittle

When I was younger, my Dad would roast peanuts in their shells (or monkey nuts as they are also called) under the glowing grill and split open the burning, charred shell to pop the toasty peanuts inside. I especially remember my Dad enjoying these one evening when I was 12, with a glass of Carling Black Label, on a day I had come home from school decidedly deflated. I recall looking at my Dad enjoying this snack and thinking how we were like any other family, despite what had taken place at school earlier that day.

Autumn was always the setting for the annual school musical and I was very excited about the prospect of being in the planned production of *Grease*. The auditions had been earlier that afternoon and I had spent all morning break and lunchtime practising a performance that I was hoping would impress the teachers. My turn arrived and I stood under the blinding spotlight on the lonely stage facing the two teachers sitting at the back of the hall, the glasses of the one on the left reflecting in the dark. I belted out a rendition of 'Hopelessly Devoted To You' and stood, breathless and hopeful, waiting for their reply. I wasn't quite prepared for what they were about to say. They conferred and then one teacher cleared her throat and said, 'You have a beautiful voice, anyone will tell you that, but I'm afraid Sandy wasn't brown and neither were any of the pink ladies. Sorry. Next!' I sat down next to my Dad and consoled myself with cracking open and munching as many peanuts as possible, which helped, temporarily.

This adaptation is a crunchy savoury brittle of peanuts still in their red skins captured in a deep-fried crispy *gram* flour and fenugreek batter net for a unique nibble. *Serves 2*

Method

1 Place the *gram* flour in a bowl and mix with enough water to make a thick batter. Add the remaining ingredients and stir well to coat.

2 Place large amounts on a perforated spoon and drop into oil to deep-fry at 170°C for 5 minutes.

½ cup gram flour

3 teaspoons dried fenugreek

½ teaspoon salt

½ teaspoon red chilli powder

200 g (7 oz) redskin peanuts

Chocolate, cardamom, coconut and pistachio barfi

The Hindu and Sikh festival of lights, Diwali (from the Sanskrit *deepavali*, meaning 'row of lights'), is fast becoming a very fashionable occasion. Last year it was mentioned in the mainstream media more than ever with the Ferreira family in *EastEnders* holding a street party in which the whole of Albert Square joined, and *The Sunday Times* 'Style' magazine even mentioned it in their stylometer as something to do in autumn.

I held a dinner party for my friends who would otherwise not get the opportunity to celebrate Diwali. So I treated these six girlies to a spread of dishes and sweets laid upon tables covered with multicoloured tissue and gold stars, in a room decorated with clusters of glittering tealights in the fireplaces and on every available surface, rose incense whispering away in the background, a screen playing the Indian film *Devdas* on mute while Nitin Sawnhey and Punjabi MC played on the stereo. I also provided cute little indoor sparklers. They were all successfuly converted to the Diwali spirit.

Mittai – our Indian sweets – are very important at Diwali and we would take trips with our parents to Leicester as children to pick up mixed boxes as a treat for ourselves and relatives and to see the Diwali lights along the Belgrave Road. Our house would be filled with incense and dozens of candles would be lit on the tables and along the windowsills. (Although I remember the house often also being very excitingly filled with candles whenever there was a thunderstorm and there would be the inevitable powercut – remember how frequent they were?)

Although Diwali is best known as the celebration of the triumph of good over evil in the form of the Hindu god Rama rescuing Sita from the evil, 10-headed demon Ravana, with the villagers lighting rows of little clay oil lamps called *dive* or *diye* (pronounced 'deev-e' or 'dee-ye') to guide them back home, this occasion has other significance as well. Diwali is also about new beginnings, or fresh starts. Hindu homes are cleaned and decorated with *rangoli* patterns in the hope of attracting the attention of the goddess Lakshmi, to welcome her into their homes. Lakshmi is the goddess of wealth and it is hoped she will bless the family with a prosperous year. Therefore, it is also a traditional time to pay off debts and tie up financial and business-related loose ends. Sweets are exchanged with friends and relatives in this spirit of renewal and goodwill.

For Sikhs, there is an additional poignant significance. The 6th Sikh Guru Hargobind Singh Ji and 52 kings were released from prison by the Mughal emperor Jahangir on the day of Diwali. The Sikhs were naturally overjoyed and so lit lamps and candles on their roofs to guide him home to Amritsar in the Punjab. His mother was so thankful to God that she gave out food and sweets to everyone in the village.

Sweets are therefore very important at Diwali and the giving of them as gifts is a highly symbolic part of the occasion. These squares of cardamom and coconut *barfi* are topped with a layer of rich chocolate and sprinkled with striking chopped pistachios. They make the perfect Diwali gift, provided you can bear to give them away. *Makes 12 large squares*

Method

1 Place the milk powder, 1 teaspoon melted butter, ¼ teaspoon green cardamom powder and the double cream in a large bowl and mix well.

2 Place the coconut and the remaining melted butter in a saucepan and fry until light brown, stirring continuously with a wooden spoon.

3 Add the milk powder mixture, sugar and remaining green cardamom powder and stir continuously on a low heat. At first, the mixture will be solid, but as you stir it will become more flexible, as the sugar dissolves with the butter, and then gradually thick and creamy.

4 Keep stirring and, when it begins to come away from the sides of the pan, stir for another 5–6 minutes so that it is nice and thick.

5 Pour on to a non-stick tray and spread into a 2.5-cm (1-inch) thick square. Use your fingers to create straight edges.

6 Break the chocolate into squares and place in a heatproof bowl over a pan of very hot water – make sure the water does not touch the bowl. Keep stirring with a wooden spoon until melted. Pour over the barfi slab, using a knife to spread it to the edges.

7 Sprinkle with pistachios.

8 Refrigerate for 4 hours and then use a sharp knife to cut into squares.

1½ cups full cream milk powder

3 teaspoons melted butter

1¼ teaspoon green cardamom powder

150 ml (¼ pint) double cream

⅓ cup medium desiccated coconut

⅓ cup granulated sugar

150 g (5½ oz) cooking chocolate

large handful chopped pistachios

Chicken biryani

Real chicken *biryani* is worlds away from the restaurant version of fairly bland chicken mixed with multicoloured rice served up with a pale brown curry sauce. In fact, when I first came across real chicken *biryani*, I was utterly shocked at just how different it was. A real *biryani* is made by layering rice with a strong meat mixture cooked with heavy, aromatic whole spices and then slow-baking it with a little milk and saffron allowing the meat to tenderise and the spices to infuse their flavour. Admittedly, this centuries-old dish is one of the longest and hardest dishes to cook.

Given the special quality of it, it is therefore one of the dishes commonly made for the Islamic Eid celebration, which marks the end of the Ramadan month of fasting. After prayer, exotic and luxurious dishes are prepared for the evening meal to be shared with friends and family, where gifts and good wishes are exchanged. The spirit of this festival is one of forgiveness, charity, thankfulness, peace and community. Food is shared on this evening according to the practice of *zakat*, which is the obligation to share food with others. However, although this is clearly a joyous occasion, it is not a time for overindulgence, frivolity or the pursuit of material pleasure. The joy derives from God having enabled people to perform their Ramadan duties.

Set aside a few hours to cook this *biryani*, which makes a very special feature dish at a dinner party, and is best served with cumin *raita*, *naan* and a side vegetable dish. *Serves 4–6*

Method

2 cups basmati rice

Rice spices

3 green and 2 brown cardamoms

5 cloves

1 teaspoon black peppercorns

1 bay leaf

1 stick cinnamon

½ teaspoon salt

½ cup oil

3 onions, finely sliced

¼ cup yogurt

3 cloves garlic, crushed

1½ teaspoons grated fresh ginger

4 green chillies, finely chopped

900 g (2 lb) diced chicken –

    white and dark meat

¼ cup canned chopped tomatoes

Meat spices

5 green cardamoms, slightly split

2 brown cardamoms

1 tablespoon cumin seeds

1 teaspoon garam masala

5 cloves

1 teaspoon black peppercorns

2 bay leaves

2 sticks cinnamon

2 teaspoons coriander powder

1½ teaspoons salt

¼ teaspoon ground nutmeg

¼ teaspoon cinnamon powder

3 tablespoons lemon juice

handful of chopped coriander

large pinch of saffron soaked in

    4 tablespoons warm milk for

    30 minutes

butter

1 Boil the rice with the rice spices (green cardamom, brown cardamom, cloves, black peppercorns, bay leaf, cinnamon stick and salt) for 5 minutes or so (it will still be underdone) and drain, retaining the spices.

2 Heat the oil in a large pan and fry the onions until a deep, dark brown. Remove the onions from the pan with a slotted spoon, placing about a fifth on a plate and the rest in a large bowl.

3 Mix the onions in the bowl with the yogurt, crushed garlic, ginger and chillies.

4 Add the chicken to the oil in the pan in which the onions were fried and stir-fry for 5 minutes until golden.

5 Turn the heat to low and add the yogurt mixture and stir well.

6 Add the tomatoes and the meat spices (green cardamom, brown cardamom, cumin, *garam masala*, cloves, black peppercorns, bay leaves, cinnamon sticks, coriander powder, salt, nutmeg and cinnamon powder) and stir well until shiny and the oil separates.

7 Turn the heat very, very low and cover and cook for 30 minutes, stirring occasionally.

8 Place a layer of the meat mixture on the bottom of a large casserole dish. Spread a layer of rice on top and then another layer of meat and finally another layer of rice.

9 Pour the lemon juice over the rice.

10 Top with the coriander and the remaining fried onion.

11 Pour over the saffron and the milk and dot with butter.

12 Cover tightly with foil and bake in an oven preheated to 180°C, Gas Mark 4, for 1 hour.

Patra pinwheel salad

I first came across this Gujarati snack at university when friends introduced me to it. *Patra* is colocasia leaves combined with oil, *gram* flour and spices and compressed. The mixture is bought in a can and emerges from it as a solid roll. You then cut the roll into circular slices, revealing the pinwheel cross-section pattern of the leaves rolled together. These are then shallow fried until crisp, golden and slightly charred. At university we used to munch this snack with ketchup but, here in this dish, it is the main ingredient in an unusual hot salad with coriander leaves and a mild yogurt and mint sauce. *Serves 2*

Method

1 Open the can and very carefully remove the *patra* roll. I do this by scoring around the roll inside the can with a long, thin sharp knife and then pushing the knife into the roll on the side facing you and gently pulling the roll out. Cut the roll into 8 slices.

2 Heat the oil in a non-stick frying pan on a medium heat. Add the slices, 4 at a time, and fry for a few minutes on each side until crisp and golden brown.

3 Serve on a bed of rocket, coriander, tomato, cucumber and spring onions and drizzle with the yogurt mixed with the mint sauce.

400 g (14 oz) can patra

2 teaspoons oil

1 packet of rocket leaves

handful of fresh coriander sprigs

2 tomatoes, diced

¼ cucumber, diced

2 spring onions, finely chopped

¼ cup natural yogurt

1 teaspoon mint sauce

Maple home fries with red chilli

I first ate home fries in a New York diner on the way to the Natural History Museum and, boy, were they good. They were served as part of a breakfast with crispy bacon, mushrooms and eggs-over-easy, and are similar to British fried potatoes. As I am exceptionally greedy I like to take on any festivals that are food-orientated and I have always been very attracted to the culinary idea of the Thanksgiving Dinner.

Although I absolutely don't agree with the origins of the occasion itself – I have too much respect for the indigenous American culture for that – I very much like the sound of turkey, yams and sweet pumpkin pie. I also like the social aspect – Thanksgiving always seems such a warm time in American movies, full of seasonal good cheer and family values, especially in those old cheesy movies that come on in the middle of the afternoon that I am a sucker for.

So I decided to create my own take on home fries, with the addition of maple syrup, wholegrain mustard and red chilli, for my own autumnal Thanksgiving-style brunch.

Incidentally, chilli, the ingredient synonymous with Indian food was actually brought to India from the New World after the voyages of Vasco da Gama. Americans, however, do not seem to have widely embraced Indian food in return. When I was in New York, I found it a real challenge to find many Indian restaurants, and even more of a challenge to find any of quality. There was one street that seemed to be a little India, comprising of about half a dozen Indian restaurants with names like 'Curry in a Hurry', as well as one very small shop with the notice 'We sell everything Indian' written on the window. And they weren't wrong. Inside, it was crammed with everything from jars of *achaar* through to Indian films to incense. Packets of *dhal* competed for space with packets of *bindia*. But, if you are ever in New York, I can highly recommend food store Dean and Deluca, who sell one of the best *garam masala* blends I have ever come across. *Serves 2–4*

Method

1 In a bowl, mix the mustard, Worcestershire sauce, soy sauce, maple syrup, salt, pepper and herbs with a spoon.

2 Heat the oil in a pan and fry the onion until lightly golden.

3 Add the potatoes and pan-fry until they begin to go golden.

4 Pour in the maple mixture and stir well, but gently, so as not to break the potatoes but to make sure that they are well covered.

5 Leave to cook for a couple of minutes, turning over occasionally, so that the potatoes are nice and brown with a crispy coating.

6 Add the chilli, stir again, and serve.

3 tablespoons wholegrain mustard

generous splash of Worcestershire sauce

generous splash of soy sauce

12 teaspoons maple syrup

salt and coarsely ground black pepper, to season

1 teaspoon dried mixed herbs

2 tablespoons mild olive oil

½ onion sliced

4 potatoes, scrubbed, cut into chunks, boiled and drained

1 large red chilli, cut into round slices

Gulab jamun

These famous cardamom flavoured, brown, fried, sponge balls in sugar syrup showered with desiccated coconut are a traditional Indian sweet served hot or cold, alone or with ice cream. Although they are widely available from Indian sweet shops, they are very easy to make at home and are just the thing to share when celebrating Sikh Gurpurb (Guru Remembrance Day), the occasion of the birthday of Guru Nanak Dev Ji.

Guru Nanak, founder of the Sikh faith, was born in 1469 in Talwandi into a deeply divided society. His message, following his enlightenment of the truth, was a simple one – there is only one God, of whom we are all children. Love for God and fellow man, combined with holistic truthful living, were pronounced as the only way to become closer to the Lord, not convoluted ritual. He preached against violence and social inequality based on caste, class, religion and gender. These teachings of unity, empathy, charity, justice and modesty are poignantly relevant in today's troubled times, and we would all benefit from taking a moment to consider them.

Guru Nanak's birthday is usually celebrated in November, in accordance with the lunar calendar. This sacred, and joyous, occasion usually lasts for 3 days with an Akhand Path held in the *gurudwara*, leading up to the day itself, while women prepare in the kitchen for the Langar. A day before, a large procession led by the Panj Piaray (five armed guards representing the five beloved ones carrying the Sikh flag) and the palanquin of the Sikh holy book, the *Shri Guru Granth Sahib*, is organised, and followed by many devotees – men, women and children – singing hymns in praise and exclaiming '*Sat Sri Akal*' (hail victory to the true Lord), accompanied by a band. This procession is called the Nagakirtan and is a colourful one decorated with flowers, flags and religious banners. On the actual Gurpurb, prayers and hymns (*kirtan*) begin very early in the morning, often followed by stories of Sikh history and poetry praising Guru Nanak. After Ardas, Karah Prasad is distributed and Langar is served to all. In the evening, Sikhs illuminate their homes with candles and lamps and occasionally fireworks are lit in a display at the *gurudwara*. Unfortunately, no display in Britain can rival the Golden Temple in Amritsar in India on this night, when with its twinkling lights it looks like a magical, floating palace shining in worship of the Guru.
Makes approx. 30

Method

1 Place the milk powder, self-raising flour, semolina, sugar and green cardamom powder in a large bowl and mix with a spoon.

2 Add the milk very slowly, mixing together with a spoon, then knead into a soft dough.

3 Half fill a large saucepan with clean sunflower or vegetable oil and heat up on a very low heat.

4 Meanwhile, roll the dough into small 2.5-cm (1-inch) diameter balls, making sure that they are completely smooth with no creases.

5 Check that the oil is hot enough by dropping a tiny amount of dough into the pan – if it rises to the top straight away, it is hot enough.

6 Place about six or seven balls into the oil, making sure they have enough room – they will expand upon cooking – and fry, turning occasionally, for about 10–12 minutes until golden brown. You will notice that they start to almost do somersaults and spin around by themselves. This is a very good sign that they are cooking all the way through.

7 While the first batch are frying, place the sugar and water for the syrup in a pan and bring to the boil, stirring to dissolve the sugar, and then turn down to a very low heat – so that the heat is just barely on. The syrup is ready when it is of one thread consistency between your thumb and forefinger.

8 Drain the first batch of *gulab jamun* onto kitchen paper and then place into the pan with the syrup – they should float. Continue until you have fried all of them.

9 Sprinkle with the coconut and either serve hot immediately or refrigerate and serve cold.

2 cups full cream milk powder

½ cup self-raising flour

1 tablespoon coarse semolina

1 tablespoon white granulated sugar

½ teaspoon green cardamom powder

⅔ cup warm full cream milk

sunflower or vegetable oil

For the syrup

2 cups white granulated sugar

3 cups cold water

small handful of desiccated coconut

Sheets of sleet panel the air, pellets of hail bomb the frozen earth,

Darkness arrives early, engulfing all with his gothic billowy shadows.

A solitary lantern is lit above a doorway, its lambency playing with the lacquered

    leaves and scarlet berries of a wreath,

Twinkling in time to the peals of laughter past the oak and stained glass divide,

The tipsy scent of mulled orange, cinnamon and clove,

Softens the astringent air...

Multicoloured pepper lamb

Winter requires hearty, substantial food and this dish is both of those things, as well as being visually stunning, injecting a little colour into an indigo evening. This moist minced lamb dish is cooked in a simple *tarka* with diced multicoloured peppers of red, green, yellow or orange. Eat it with *roti* and *achaar* or on top of jacket potatoes. Alternatively, you can place this lamb in an ovenware dish, top with a cheesy mash and bake in the oven for a spicy variety of shepherd's pie that children will love, especially those feeling a little weak from seasonal colds and 'flu.

I used to be a nightmare as a child when I was ill, so my mother would dread the annual winter onslaught of sniffles, coughs, aches, pains and temperatures. I would scream until I cried when having my inoculations at the doctors: the poor receptionist had to explain to startled patients in the waiting room that I was just having a jab, and not being murdered. Feeding me medicine had to be planned with military precision: I needed at least half an hour's notice to psyche myself up, during which time I put considerable effort into trying to persuade my Mum I didn't need the dreaded, gloopy, gag-inducing, mauve Calpol or the dark, blood red, bitter Sudafed. Medicine-feeding would always take place next to the sink, should I involuntarily be sick, and a drink, biscuit and tissue were required to be close at hand to aid in the post-consumption melodrama.

Although my Mum clearly despaired of this ridiculous behaviour, she was very patient. However, I learned my lesson during the winter when I was five years old. I was suffering from tonsilitis and had a hospital appointment scheduled for an operation to take them out. I had missed quite a bit of school and so the headteacher, Mrs Jacobs, sent her secretary trundling through the snow to our house with a ginormous box full of assorted goodies, including sherbet lemons, pear drops, flying saucers, swirly lollipops, wax crayons and even an exquisite Chinese folded paper fan with a swishy black tassle. It was overwhelmingly generous. The night before the operation, as I was reading in bed, tucked up in my new pyjamas bought especially for the occasion, the nurse came to give me a dose of some vivid orange medicine. It was served in a large plastic cup and she very firmly told me to drink it all up at once. As soon as she had left the ward I sneaked to the bathroom and spat out this vile elixir, having refused to swallow it. I remember smiling to myself smugly as I got back into bed. The next morning, I was wheeled along to the operating theatre, my Mum at my side, comforting me in my state of panic. They placed a mask upon my face and asked me to count back from 10. I got to 1 and lay there, blinking, staring at the doctors, confused as to what they required me to do next. A frenzy of activity ensued as they tried to work out why I wasn't falling asleep. Then I heard them mention the medicine I was supposedly administered the night before. Frightened by all the commotion, I burst into tears and blurted out that I had spat it out into the sink. The doctors were highly unimpressed by this confession and one of them said, in a very stern manner, 'Well, you'll just have to have an injection instead then' and unceremoniously stabbed me with a very painful needle. That taught me. *Serves 4–6*

Method

1 Heat the oil in a large pan with the cumin seeds. When they begin to sizzle, add the onion and garlic and fry until quite a deep golden brown.

2 Remove the pan from the heat for a few seconds and add the tomatoes, ginger, chillies, salt, *garam masala*, turmeric and a handful of coriander. Adding a splash of water if necessary, cook on a low heat until the mixture becomes shiny and the oil separates.

3 Add the mince and stir thoroughly to coat. Add the peppers and potatoes and stir thoroughly again. Stir-fry for a few minutes.

4 Add a cup of water, stir, and bring to the boil. Cover and simmer on a low heat for 20 minutes.

5 Remove the lid, turn the heat up and stir-fry for a couple of minutes. The lamb should be nice and moist but there should be no water left.

6 Scatter a handful of chopped coriander over the top.

2 tablespoons oil

1 teaspoon cumin seeds

1 onion, finely chopped

2 cloves garlic, finely chopped

½ cup canned chopped tomatoes

2 teaspoons grated fresh ginger

3 green chillies, finely chopped

1½ teaspoons salt

1 teaspoon garam masala

½ teaspoon ground turmeric

2 handfuls of chopped coriander

450 g (1 lb) lean minced lamb

3 peppers of different colours –
I use one red, one green, one
yellow, diced

1 potato, peeled, diced and
washed

Karahi Chicken

This speciality chicken dish originates from Pakistan where it is cooked in a special metal utensil, called a *karahi*, and stir-fried on a high heat; the fresh ingredients are chopped and added, often right in front of the eager customers. You can use a wok or large frying pan and, as long as you cook it with a bit of gusto, you'll be fine. Small pieces of chicken breast are added to a bubbling mixture of ginger, garlic, green chilli, tomato and turmeric then tossed around on a high heat with fresh ginger sticks, onion, peppers and coriander, retaining all the fresh flavour. Serve with fluffy *naan* bread to mop up the tantalising juices of this steamy dish, hot enough to thaw the iciest of weather. *Serves 4*

Method

½ cup oil

1 tablespoon grated fresh ginger

1 tablespoon crushed garlic

4 green chillies, finely chopped

3 tomatoes, chopped

½ teaspoon ground turmeric

800 g (1 lb 12 oz) diced chicken
    breast

2.5-cm (1-inch) piece of fresh
    ginger, cut into thin sticks

3 teaspoons garam masala

1 teaspoon salt

½ onion, sliced

1 green pepper, thinly sliced

2 tomatoes, quartered

squeeze of lime

large handful chopped coriander

1 Heat the oil in a large frying pan, wok or *karahi* and add the grated ginger and garlic. Stirring continuously, fry until golden brown and then add the chillies, chopped tomatoes and ground turmeric.

2 When the oil has separated out, add the chicken and stir-fry until the chicken is cooked and lightly golden.

3 Continuing to stir-fry, add the ginger sticks, *garam masala*, salt and ½ cup of water and keep stirring until you have a little, thick, rich sauce.

4 Add the onion, pepper and tomatoes and stir-fry very quickly on a high heat so the vegetables are just slightly softened.

5 Add a squeeze of lime and the coriander, stir and switch off the heat.

Marrow with fenugreek and shallots

This is one of the *sabjia* I like to make during the Christmas season for relatives who prefer Indian food. It is especially good for Christmas Eve evening *roti*. It has a rich flavour with chunks of marrow softened with whole rustic shallots, flavoured with plentiful, dark, fresh fenugreek leaves. I recommend using a non-stick pan for this and whatever you do, don't add any water. The first time I made this I added water, completely forgetting that marrow releases a lot of water of its own, and so it turned into a sort of soup, resulting in me rather frantically calling my Mum into the kitchen to help fix it. Which, of course, she did. *Serves 4–6*

Method

1 Heat the oil in a non-stick pan and add the onion and garlic. Fry until golden brown.

2 Remove the pan from the heat for a few seconds and add the tomatoes, chillies, ginger, salt, *garam masala* and turmeric and stir well. Do not add any extra water. When the mixture becomes shiny and the oil separates out, add the fenugreek leaves and cook, stirring, for 1 minute.

3 Add the marrow and shallots and stir thoroughly to coat. Do not add any extra water, as you would when cooking the majority of *sabjia*, as the marrow will release water upon cooking.

4 Cover and steam through on a low heat for 20 minutes.

5 Sprinkle with the coriander.

2 tablespoons oil

1 large onion, finely chopped

2 cloves garlic, finely chopped

½ cup canned chopped tomatoes

2 green chillies, finely chopped

2 teaspoons grated fresh ginger

1½ teaspoons salt

2 teaspoons garam masala

1 teaspoon turmeric powder

2 large handfuls of fresh fenugreek leaves, finely chopped

1 marrow (850 g/1 lb 14 oz), cut into medium-sized chunks

1 packet of shallots (250 g), skinned and kept whole

handful of chopped coriander

Zeera chicken wings

If there is one dish in this book that you simply must try, it is this one. Incredibly easy and yet by far one of the most delicious things I have ever eaten. A generous helping of cumin seeds are added to plenty of scorching hot oil, to which is then added garlic, ginger and chicken wings. Chilli flakes, lemon juice and coriander powder enhance the flavour of the crunchy, dusky, cumin crust of these wings that are part fried and part steamed.

In fact, a friend who ate my first batch requested the recipe immediately, promising to keep it a secret for the time being, and cooked it at a dinner party for friends who also loved it and queried how to make it for themselves. The recipe quickly began to circulate by word of mouth – the very best way.

Eat as a snack or with rice or breads, with lots of salad and yogurt. My recipe uses skinned chicken wings but you can use boneless pieces of chicken too. Furthermore, you can increase the quantities and use skinned chicken drumsticks too. *Serves 2*

Method

1 Heat the oil in a large pan with the cumin seeds. When they begin to sizzle, add the ginger and garlic. Turn the heat low and keep stirring until golden.

2 Add the chicken and the remaining ingredients and stir-fry until well coated.

3 Cover and cook on a very low heat for 30 minutes, stirring gently; turn the chicken over halfway through the cooking time.

4 Drain almost all of the oil away (tip the pan to pour it out) and then stir-fry on a high heat for 1 minute and serve.

1 cup oil

3 tablespoons cumin seeds

2 teaspoons crushed garlic

2 teaspoons grated fresh ginger

450 g (1 lb) skinned chicken wings

1 teaspoon salt

¼ teaspoon red chilli powder

2 teaspoons coriander powder

½ teaspoon dried red chilli flakes

2 tablespoons lemon juice

Advent bombs

These festive canapés were created for a Christmas party where I wanted to combine British and Indian flavours in a way that was also visually striking. These bombs not only taste incredible but, when stacked on top of each other in a pyramid-style formation like in the Ferrero Rocher ad, you will definitely be the hostess with the mostest, and all your guests will be praising your party-giving talents, insisting that 'With these bombs you are spoiling us'.

The 'bombs', as I have nicknamed them, are Indian *golgappe*, also known as *pani puri*, and are very delicate, golden, deep-fried, hollow spheres of the most fragile pastry, which can be bought ready-made in packs of various sizes from Indian shops and sweet stores. I bought two packs of 50 for the party. Although it can be a little tedious, and slightly crazy making, to carefully tap away a hole in the top of each one, with the very tip of your finger, in order to fill them, they are worth the hassle and are a winner just on presentation alone.

I chose two varieties of filling: wintery goat's cheese, apricots, pine nuts and rosemary for the first, and traditional sage and onion, chestnuts, crispy bacon, mushrooms and cranberries for the second. The fillings are also great spread on top of bruschetta, lightly grilled and served as a Christmas lunch starter. *Makes 100*

Method

1 For filling one, toast the pine nuts in a dry non-stick frying pan by stirring them continuously until they are golden brown.

2 Place them in a large bowl with the potatoes and apricots. Roughly crumble the goat's cheese into the bowl.

3 Divide the rosemary in half and place the leaves of one half in a pestle and mortar and bash to release the aroma. Add to the mixture.

4 Add the herbs, salt and pepper and mix well.

5 For filling two, prepare both variants of stuffing in two bowls as per the packet instructions (adding boiling water and leaving to soak) and also add a knob of butter and a small dash of malt vinegar to each bowl.

6 Meanwhile, gently fry the bacon, mushrooms and onion in a frying pan. If you add the bacon first, you shouldn't need to add any extra oil as the fat from the bacon will be plenty, and the mushrooms will release a little water. Fry until the bacon is nice and crisp and the mushrooms and onions are softened.

7 Place both stuffings together in a large bowl and add the bacon, mushrooms and onions. Season with salt and pepper and mix well.

8 Grease two large baking trays and place each type of filling on a tray.

9 Bake in an oven preheated to 200°C, Gas Mark 6, for about 30 minutes until browned on top. Mix with a fork and leave to cool at room temperature.

10 Take a *puri/golgappa* and place on a plate. Using your index finger, and your nail, tap away a hole in the centre. The best way to do this is to tap a little hole and then tap around it in a circular motion to widen it. Using a tiny teaspoon, place a little of filling one into the bomb to fill it up so that it is coming a little out of the hole. Garnish with a couple of rosemary leaves poked in. Continue until all 50 bombs are completed and display on a tray, stacked on top of each other like profiteroles if you like.

11 Make holes in each of the second batch of 50 *puris/golpappe* and fill with filling number two. This time, top each hole with a little cranberry sauce. Display on trays.

Filling one

1 large bag of pine nuts

4 potatoes, peeled, diced, boiled and drained

1 bag of dried apricots, finely chopped

4 blocks of crumbly Welsh goat's cheese

1 packet fresh rosemary

2 tablespoons dried mixed herbs

salt and coarsely ground black pepper, to season

Filling two

1 packet of sage and onion stuffing

1 packet of chestnut stuffing

butter

dash of malt vinegar

1 packet of streaky bacon, snipped into small pieces

1 packet of mushrooms, diced

1 red onion, finely chopped

salt and coarsely ground black pepper, to season

1 bottle cranberry jelly with whole, plump cranberries

2 boxes each of 50 pani puris/golgappe

Mini cranberry tikkia

The *aloo tikkia* in my first book have created quite a fuss and now seem to have their own dedicated following and fan base. Every single person I have made them for has become truly addicted (I often make them for friends to cheer them up when they are down or feeling unwell) and they then go off on a crusade to get as many people to try them as possible.

Here is a special Christmas variation. Tiny little *tikkia* of potato flavoured with *garam masala*, chilli, cumin and pomegranate seed powder are given the seasonal addition of chopped cranberries for that extra tangy bite. The most important thing to remember when making these is to use a good finely ground pomegranate seed powder (or lemon juice if you can't find any) to add the right level of sourness, and also to make sure that you chop the cranberries very finely so they are not bitter.

Tikkia are named as such after the Indian word for the little pendant that Indian women often wear along their centre parting. These little patties are shaped like these tiny pendants and, I'm sure you'll agree, are certainly little gems.

Serve as Christmas nibbles at a party with some mulled wine or egg nog or as a Christmas lunch starter with a few rocket leaves and some caramelised onion chutney. *Makes 26*

Method

1 tablespoon oil

1 teaspoon cumin seeds

½ onion, finely chopped

½ teaspoon anardhana
  (pomegranate seed powder)

1 teaspoon garam masala

1½ teaspoons salt

1 teaspoon dried red chilli flakes

handful of chopped coriander

4 potatoes, peeled, boiled and
  mashed

¼ cup frozen cranberries, thawed
  and finely chopped

1 cup gram flour

1 Heat the oil in a frying pan and add the cumin seeds. When sizzling, add the onion and fry until translucent.

2 Add the pomegranate seed powder, *garam masala*, salt, chilli and coriander and stir well for about a minute.

3 Switch off the heat and add the mashed potato to the pan. Mash well with the spices. Place in a bowl and chill for 30 minutes. Add the cranberries and lightly mix.

4 Place the gram flour in a bowl and add enough water, by adding slowly and stirring continuously, to make a thick smooth batter.

5 Roll the mixture into 26 little patties. Coat each generously with the batter, using a pastry brush to dab and pat, rather than brush, both sides of each patty.

6 Shallow fry – in just enough oil to coat the bottom of the pan – in batches for about 3–4 minutes on the first side and then turning over for about 1–2 minutes.

7 Drain on kitchen paper and serve.

Spicy sprouts with cumin and mango

The majority of British Asians love celebrating Christmas. My family in particular really look forward to Christmas and it is, without a doubt, my favourite occasion of the year. Yep, I love all that seasonal sentimentality. My Mum recently told me a story about when she was at a supermarket one Christmas, when I was a teenager, stocking up on some Christmas essentials. She bumped into a colleague from work who said to her, almost sympathetically, 'You don't celebrate Christmas do you, being Indian?' My Mum said that had her colleague bothered to glance at my Mum's shopping trolley, piled high with turkey, mince pies, crackers, chipolatas, streaky bacon, stuffing, sprouts, chocolates, biscuits, Christmas cake, Christmas pudding, custard and rolls of wrapping paper emblazoned with snowmen and Santa Claus, she would have realised that this presumption was far from correct.

We would always have a real build-up to Christmas, even having presents on Christmas Eve sometimes, and would, of course, be bought advent calendars each year. I'll never forget the Christmas when my Mum bought my brother and I a Cadbury's chocolate one – each of the 24 doors a flimsy barrier to a chunky, sugary treat. However, to my disappointment, there was nothing behind door number 2, or number 3, or numbers 4, 5 and 6. My very young, cunning brother had mischieviously pilfered all the chocolates, when no one was looking (shortly after door number 1 had revealed its contents) and painstakingly closed the doors back to look as though they had never been touched to avoid being told off. It wasn't his fault, he has PWS (Prader-Willi Syndrome, the symptoms of which include an involuntary urge to eat constantly and a lack of appetite suppressant), but I wasn't so understanding at the time!

I discovered recently that turkeys were actually taken to India by the colonial British for traditional Christmas lunch. However, it didn't fare well there, being considered too dry, and the succulent peacock was apparently adopted for these festivities instead.

If we are having Christmas lunch with relatives, there will usually be two menus: one Indian and one traditional English – with many of us opting for both. Pigs in blankets nestling next to a helping of *sabji* on our heaving plates! This Brussels sprout *sabji* with cumin and mango powder is a great way to use the seasonal vegetable in a way that is suitable for the Indian palate. It was made especially for my Nan (Mum) who came to stay with us last Christmas and who is a strict vegetarian. However, this way, with a paper hat sitting jauntily upon her white-haired head, she was very much able to join in with the seasonal feast.

Serves 4

Method

1 Heat the oil in a pan and add the cumin seeds.

2 When the cumin seeds are sizzling, add the onion and garlic and fry until a light golden brown.

3 Take the pan off the heat for a few seconds and then add the tomatoes and return to a low heat. Add the chilli, ginger, lemon juice, salt, *garam masala*, turmeric powder, mango powder, coriander and a splash of water.

4 When the mixture has become shiny and the oil has separated out, add the sprouts and stir thoroughly to coat, adding ⅓ cup of water.

5 Cover and cook on a low heat for 15 minutes.

2 tablespoons oil

4 tablespoons cumin seeds

1 onion, finely chopped

1 clove garlic, finely chopped

¼ cup canned chopped tomatoes

1 green chilli, finely chopped

1 teaspoon grated fresh ginger

splash of lemon juice

1 teaspoon salt

1 teaspoon garam masala

½ teaspoon turmeric powder

1 teaspoon amchoor (dried mango powder)

handful of chopped coriander

600 g (1 lb 5 oz) sprouts, outer layers removed and halved

Masala roast potatoes

Christmas is indeed a magical time for me. The house is full of twinkling decorations, the tree stands grand with a hundred blinking stars, dotted with angels, candy canes and pine cones, tinsel wreathes the banisters, poinsettas bloom in pots on the table and musical candlesticks gently hum 'Jingle bells' in the background. When I was very little we would cut gift tags out of last year's cards, hole-punching the squares in the corner and threading them with red or gold ribbon. We would also make decorations, cutting patterns out of card and covering them with seasonal gift wrap then hanging them from the ceiling and looping home-made paper chains around the walls. Of course, we had shop-bought decorations too but it was so special for my brother and I to spend hours making these with our parents and added to the building excitement for the big day.

My Dad used to be a photographer and a cameraman for the BBC before he sacrificed it and chose IT as a career more suitable to support a young family. Owing to this love for the camera, my whole childhood is recorded on numerous, extremely amusing, home video tapes. My brother and I would spend Saturday evenings singing songs or miming along to Indian soundtracks, with matching dance routines, often in the garden, next to neighbours who were now used to it all and quite liked these colourful entertaining displays. We would put on a show while my Dad perfected camera techniques and we thoroughly enjoyed it, always happy to oblige.

All special occasions were filmed, and all our relatives used to join in too. Although it wasn't the done thing to sing or dance in public, it was perfectly harmless within your own four walls for fun. At birthday parties we would often be treated to a song from my *Chachaji*, who is a great singer and has more singing, acting and dancing talent than most of the Indian film industry put together, and is without a doubt the star of the family. The camera was simply another member of the family, which most of the time was fine, but I remember one particular incident when I didn't like the camera so much. It was Christmas morning when I was four years old and my Dad came into the bedroom to wake me up, a camera in front of his face. 'Vicky, it's Christmas, wake up.' I woke up excited, rubbing my eyes and bounded straight to the living room where a mountain of presents were waiting under the tree. Just before I got to them my Dad said, 'Wait, go back, that wasn't quite right, we need to take that again.' So I went back, pretended to be asleep and we repeated the scene. By the tenth time of doing this, I just wanted my presents! The funniest thing is that none of the videos are edited, so there I am just going forwards and backwards, never quite getting to the presents until we finally got it right. But those presents were worth the delay. We were thoroughly

spoilt as my parents would spend money they couldn't really afford on piles and piles of gifts for us.

I make these potatoes often and they are great for adding a little subtle spice to your traditional Christmas meal. I made them one Christmas when we had my Nan (Mum), Bindi Massi, David Mamma, Mammi, Bali Massi and my cousins Nicky, Shindy, Sapphire and Areese over. They went down very well and a darn sight better than the television programming that year, which I remember as being so dire that we all thought it better to go to the cinema instead. *Serves 2*

Method

1 Preheat oven to 230°C, Gas Mark 8.

2 Boil the potatoes until soft and drain.

3 Turn into a baking tray and toss with the remaining ingredients, making sure the potatoes are well coated with the butter and have mashed slightly on the outside.

4 Roast in the oven until golden and crispy, about 25 minutes.

2 large potatoes, peeled, cut into large chunks and washed

2 garlic cloves, unpeeled

large knob of butter

generous sprinkle of garam masala

generous sprinkle of cumin powder

good grind of sea salt

Aubergine bartha

This smoky aubergine dish – one of my Dad's favourites – is currently enjoying somewhat of a revival in our house at the moment. The aubergines are oven roasted in their skins and then the velvety flesh is scooped out and added to a seductive *tarka* of cassia bark, garlic and cinnamon, mashed until it is a steamed purée that is a joy to eat with any form of bread at any time and is especially good for a light Boxing Day lunch. You can also combine some with yogurt for a wintery dip.

The first time I made this, I placed several aubergines in the oven and then went to clean the bathroom, thinking everything would be fine as the oven was on a timer. Not long after, I heard a small explosion. In my absentmindedness, I had forgotten to pierce the aubergines and they had thus exploded, coating the whole oven in flesh, skin and seeds. As I gingerly explained to my Mum that I thought I'd stabbed them, I thought she'd stab me! However, she was surprisingly calm as she cleaned the entire oven, despite my offers to do it. So, please, remember to stab the aubergines! *Serves 2–5*

Method

2 large aubergines

3 tablespoons oil

1 teaspoon cumin seeds

1 small stick cassia bark

1 onion, thinly sliced

2 cloves garlic, finely chopped

¼ cup canned chopped tomatoes

1 teaspoon salt

1 teaspoon garam masala

1 teaspoon cinnamon powder

**2 green chillies, finely chopped
with seeds**

handful of chopped coriander

1 tablespoon grated ginger

¼ red onion, thinly sliced

stick of cinnamon

1   Stab the aubergines several times place on a baking tray and bake in an oven pre-heated to 220°C, Gas Mark 7, for 1 hour, turning over halfway through the cooking time. Cut in half lengthways and scoop out the flesh.

2   Heat the oil in a pan and add the cumin seeds and cassia bark. When the cumin is sizzling, add the onion (not red onion) and garlic and fry until golden brown.

3   Take the pan off the heat for a few seconds and then add the tomato, salt, *garam masala*, cinnamon powder, chillies, coriander and ginger. Return to a low heat and stir until shiny and the oil separates.

4   Add the aubergine flesh and mix well, mashing lightly.

5   Add ⅓ cup of water, stir gently, cover and steam through on a very low heat for 15 minutes.

6   Garnish with the red onion and cinnamon stick.

Deep-fried amchoor okra

Make the most of the gluttonous holiday season (before embarking upon the inevitable diet) with these deep-fried okra slices, liberally seasoned with sour dried mango powder. My sister loves these and quickly discovered, upon first tasting them, that they go down dangerously easily. Keep in mind too that the halved okra shrink in size quite dramatically when fried so be sure to make more than you think you'll need.

Serves 4

Method

1 Wash and dry the okra. It is very important that the okra is dried thoroughly as otherwise it will become very sticky when you cut it.

2 Slice each okra in half lengthways.

3 Heat the oil in a deep-fryer to 170°C.

4 Deep-fry the okra in batches for about 4–5 minutes until golden and crispy.

5 Drain on kitchen paper and dust with mango powder and salt.

large bag of okra, about 50

oil

amchoor (dried mango powder)

salt

Rainbow cocktails

If you are holding a New Year's Eve party and want to impress your guests, these amazing cocktails – alcoholic or non-alcoholic as you wish – are a sure-fire way to earn yourself domestic goddess status.

Tall champagne glasses, with snowy sugar-frosted rims are lined up in rows on a table or counter, each row containing half a glass of the following fruit purées: red raspberry and strawberry, orange mandarins, yellow pineapple, green kiwi, indigo blueberry and purple blackberries – all the rainbow spectrum. The visual impact is nothing short of stunning. They are then topped up with champagne or non-alcoholic spritzer as required for the enjoyment of your guests, served with a little swizzle stick.

They couldn't be simpler – all you need is a blender and the purées can be made in advance and stored in containers in the fridge, leaving you to enjoy the party too. Remember, the way you spend New Year's Eve is the way you'll spend the rest of the year, so spend it in style. *Makes 84*

Method

½ cup lemon juice

2 cups white granulated sugar

2 punnets of raspberries, blended

1 large punnet strawberries, stalks removed and halved, blended

2 cans of mandarins, drained of liquid, blended

2 cans of crushed pineapple, drained of excess liquid, blended

6 kiwi fruits, peeled and diced, blended

2 punnets of blueberries, blended with a little extra water

2 cans blackberries, drained of liquid, blended

4–6 large bottles of champagne or non-alcoholic sparkling spritzer

1 Pour the lemon juice into a large dish or deep plate and pour the sugar on to another plate. Take each of the 84 champagne flutes and dip the rims into the lemon juice and then into the sugar to give a crystallised rim.

2 Divide the fruit purées among the glasses, so each glass is about half full, so that you have 12 of each of the seven rainbow colours. Arrange on a table or surface so that you have the rows of the rainbow colours going across horizontally.

3 Top the glasses with champagne or spritzer and enjoy!

Mini black forest samose

Samose, triangular-shaped deep-fried pastries are usually filled with potatoes and peas, shredded chicken or minced lamb, but can also be made with a sweet filling. These sophisticated baby *samose* are filled with gothic shards of rich, dark, Belgian chocolate and chopped black cherries and served with a dollop of thick, whipped cream for a spectacular sweet to serve at a New Year's Eve party. *Makes 84*

Method

1 Place one cup of flour in a large shallow bowl and add the salt and oil. Mix with your hands and then add water very, very slowly, kneading at the same time, until you have a firm, smooth dough. Cover with cling film or place in a sealed container and refrigerate for a minimum of 15 minutes.

2 Mix the chocolate and cherries in a bowl and refrigerate. Make sure the chocolate does not have very sharp edges, which could tear the pastry.

3 Mix together the remaining flour with enough water to make a thick sticky paste. Try to get the lumps out but do not make it too thick or too runny. This will be your glue to hold the *samose* together.

4 Rinse the *thawa* and put it on a very low heat. Take the dough out of the fridge and place the container on the worktop next to the *thawa*. Place next to it some more oil in a little bowl with a teaspoon in it. Place a clean tea towel that has been folded in half widthways on a tea plate. Get out a small, sharp knife. Dust some flour on a large plate or chopping board.

5 Divide the dough into 10 balls, each 2.5 cm (1 inch) in diameter, and roll the first out a little, to make a small disc. Repeat this with a second ball, making sure it is the same size as the first.

6 Take the first disc and dip in the flour. Shake off any excess. Place it flat on the work surface. Using the teaspoon, spread a little oil on the surface and sprinkle with a tiny amount of flour. Place the second disc on top and lightly press the edges to seal. Turn over and press again.

7 Dip both sides in the flour, shaking off any excess, and roll out to the size of a saucer. Keep dipping in flour if necessary – it mustn't stick. The pastry must be very smooth and cannot have any creases in it. It needs to be flat and even so that it splits cleanly.

1½ cups plain flour, plus extra for rolling

pinch of salt

1½ teaspoons oil – the same type of oil you will be using to deep-fry

400 g (14 oz) black cherries, stoned and finely chopped (you can use canned or frozen, defrosted)

300 g (10½ oz) plain Belgian chocolate, very finely chopped

8 Pat off any excess flour and place on the *thawa*. Cook for 3 seconds on each side and then transfer to the plate. Fold in half and cut a tiny slit at the halfway mark on the edge. Open out and cut in half. Very slowly and carefully peel the two layers of each half apart. You should be left with four semicircles of pastry. Open the tea towel and place the pastry immediately on the tea towel. Cover with the other half of the tea towel to keep warm.

9 Repeat the process until you have 20 semicircles, all covered by the tea towel.

10 Take one of the semicircles of pastry (keeping the rest covered until needed) and, using your middle finger, put some of the 'glue' all around the edges of the side that looks more cooked. Hold the semicircle with the straight edge facing upwards and fold the outer left-hand corner down towards the middle of the curved edge (but do not let it touch the curved edge). Bring the right-hand corner down and seal where they both meet, overlapping slightly. You should be holding an upside-down cone.

11 Turn the cone the right way up and, holding it gently, fill to two-thirds full with the chocolate and cherry mixture. Seal the edges at the top together with your fingers so that the line where the *samosa* is sealed runs straight down the middle, adding more glue if necessary. Gently pat to even out the mixture inside.

12 When they are all filled, deep-fry them in oil heated to 170°C until golden brown and crisp (about 5–6 minutes), turning every minute with a perforated spoon.

13 Drain on kitchen paper and serve.

Garlic masala mushrooms

These are another lovely deep-fried snack best enjoyed before you begin to be calorie cautious again. Whole chestnut mushrooms are rubbed with olive oil, crushed garlic, dried coriander and *garam masala*; all the flavours are massaged in, before the mushrooms are dipped in a coriander and *gram* flour batter and fried until crisp. Eat as soon as they are cooked, dipping each mushroom into a little dish of garlic butter. A great little snack to savour while deliberating over which New Year's resolutions to make, or break. *Serves 4*

Method

1 tablespoon mild olive oil

2 cloves garlic, crushed

2 teaspoons dried coriander

salt and garam masala, to season

250 g (9 oz) whole chestnut mushrooms, washed

1 cup gram flour

handful of chopped coriander

5 tablespoons butter

1 clove garlic crushed

salt and pepper to season

1 In a large bowl, combine the olive oil, crushed garlic, dried coriander, salt and *garam masala*. Add the mushrooms and rub in the mixture.

2 Combine the gram flour and chopped coriander with enough water in a bowl to make a thick, smooth batter.

3 Dip the mushrooms into the batter and deep-fry, in batches, in oil heated to 160°C for about 4 minutes until crispy and golden. Drain.

4 Mix the butter with the garlic and salt and pepper.

5 Serve the hot mushrooms and dip into the garlic butter.

Caramelised onion chutney

This sticky, amber, almost toffee-ish chutney is full of sweet flavour. Slivers of onion are softened and caramelised with sugar, ginger, red chilli, tamarind and cinnamon. Serve hot with any main meal as a change from mango chutney or refrigerate and use as a sandwich spread. *Makes a tubful*

Method

1 Heat the oil in a pan and add the onions and ginger. Stir-fry until the onions are golden.

2 Add the sugar, turn the heat low and continue to stir to caramelise the onions.

3 Add the cinnamon, chillies, tamarind water and salt and stir-fry for a couple of minutes. Serve immediately.

2 teaspoons oil

2 large onions, sliced

1 teaspoon grated fresh ginger

2 teaspoons sugar

pinch of cinnamon powder

4 red chillies, chopped

**1 tablespoon tamarind water
   (2.5-cm/1-inch) piece block
   tamarind, soaked and broken
   down in a little boiling water
   for 30 minutes)**

$^1\!/_2$ teaspoon salt

Whole spice egg-fried rice

I was 15 years old when it first occurred to me. We were driving home in the evening after a family day out. As the car gently snaked its way through the roads of our town, I looked out of the car window up at the blinking lights of restaurant and takeaway signs shimmering in the twilight. I already knew from insider knowledge that Indian restaurant food was very different to our home food. But was this true of other ethnic groups? Was it the same with, say, Chinese food?

Although this niggling thought always remained at the back of my mind, it wasn't until last year that it was brought to my attention again. I was standing in the queue for the changing rooms at H&M in London. Collapsing under the strain of at least 16 items of clothing, which I had somehow managed to drape over both arms, I waited impatiently in what seemed to be the longest queue of my life. Unintentionally, I tuned in to the conversation of the two girls in front of me. They seemed to be young students, wearing funky clothes, had English accents and looked of Chinese ethnicity. The taller girl was excitedly suggesting dinner plans to the other, 'After this, you know what we should do? We should go and get crispy duck, proper crispy duck! Yeah, I know! There's this place and it does proper home-style Chinese food, not like all the other restaurants. All the Chinese people go there, you'll love it.'

I only just managed to restrain myself from tossing the clothes in the air and triumphantly shouting 'Aha! I knew it!' by mentally reminding myself that I was in a public place, and so carried on eavesdropping. I was then about to interrupt the conversation and ask the girl more about this but, at that moment, their turn came in the queue and my window of opportunity was lost as they disappeared into the cubicles, with a swish of long black hair.

We love Chinese food in our house and frequently treat ourselves to a takeaway from the local Mr Tangs. While I continue in my earnest quest of discovering real Chinese recipes (a Chinese girl I recently spoke to while researching this told me that, in some restaurants, Chinese customers are automatically given an entirely different menu to non-Chinese patrons), try this original version of egg-fried rice. This dish is a combination of the much-loved favourite but given a twist with buttery Indian whole spice flavours. It is just the thing to celebrate Chinese New Year. I love Chinatown in London and the dragon processions during Chinese New Year are wonderful. I hope you find this rice wonderful too. *Serves 2*

Method

1 Heat the butter in a wok or frying pan on a low heat and add all the spices.

2 Once the cumin seeds have begun to sizzle, add the peas and stir-fry for one minute.

3 Add the rice and stir-fry until lightly golden.

4 Make some space in the wok or frying pan by either pushing the rice to one side or by making a well in the centre, and pour in the egg. Leave for a few seconds and then use a fork to break up the egg – like you would for scrambled egg – and toss it around with the rice.

5 Make sure the egg is evenly distributed and serve immediately.

5 tablespoons butter

½ teaspoon whole black peppercorns

3 cloves

¼ teaspoon cumin seeds

¼ teaspoon dried red chilli flakes

2 cinnamon sticks, snapped in half

1 teaspoon salt

3 whole green cardamom pods

pinch of ground nutmeg

1 teaspoon garam masala

½ cup frozen peas

1 cup rice, boiled

2 large eggs, beaten

Naan bread

Everyone loves this bread served in Indian restaurants everywhere. They can be tricky to make at home as the restaurants place the rolled *naans* on to little pillows, which they then use to stick the *naan* to the inside of the *tandoor*. However, the following method works very well, but remember to use a high heat. Nigella seeds, the black seeds on *naans* that you will be familiar with, can be difficult to find, so just omit them if they are unavailable. Keep the *naan* warm in a clean towel or foil until ready to serve with a wide variety of dishes. *Makes 2*

Method

1 Place the flour and salt in a large bowl and mix. Add enough warm water, bit by bit, until you have a firm dough – but do not over knead. Cover and leave at room temperature, or in an airing cupboard, overnight.

2 Gently knead the dough again a little and halve. Roll and pull each half into a teardrop-shaped *naan*, about 5 mm (¼ inch) thick, and prick the uppermost side with a fork. Sprinkle with some nigella seeds.

3 Place on a preheated hot non-stick frying pan and cook until the underside is brown, about 2 minutes.

4 Place the *naan* on a grill and grill on a high heat for a couple of minutes until browned.

5 Smear with butter and wrap in foil while making the second *naan*.

2 cups self-raising flour

pinch of salt

½ cup warm water

sprinkle of kalonji (nigella seeds)

butter

Black-eyed peas sabji

No, not an ode to one of my favourite bands but a rustic, traditional *sabji* made from dried black-eyed peas and potatoes. This filling, earthy *sabji* is just the thing to enjoy with hot, fresh *rotia* for the Punjabi winter festival of Lohri, celebrated by Hindus and Sikhs alike. The night of the Lohri celebration is believed to be the coldest of the year, and in India the festivities traditionally take place around bonfires. This event has a special significance for families with a newborn or newly-married son, as popcorn, sesame and rice flakes are thrown into the fire for good luck and health. This practice continues to take place among British Asians. Young brides, for whome Lohri is considered very important, are encouraged to throw special black sesame seeds into the flames, as it is believed she will have as many sons as the seeds she throws into the fire. Although Sikhism promotes equality between sons and daughters, old cultural beliefs result in an unfortunate continuing, although declining, preference for sons rather than daughters. Daughters were considered a financial burden in the olden days but now, with women working and able to contribute to the household income and their wedding costs, this is no longer a reality. *Makes 4–6*

Method

1 Heat the oil in a large pan and add the onion and garlic. Fry until golden brown.

2 Remove the pan from the heat for a few seconds and then add the tomatoes, ginger, chillies, salt, turmeric powder, *garam masala* and half the coriander.

3 Stir well and cook on a low heat until the mixture becomes shiny and the oil separates out. Add the drained peas and stir-fry on a higher heat until well coated. Add the potatoes and also stir-fry until evenly coated with the mixture.

4 Add enough water to just cover the peas and potatoes, including the water the peas were soaked in; bring to the boil and then cover and simmer for 20 minutes.

5 Remove the lid and turn up the heat to thicken the sauce a little for about 1 minute. Switch off the heat and sprinkle with the remaining coriander.

2 tablespoons oil

1 onion, finely chopped

1 clove garlic, finely chopped

1 cup canned chopped tomatoes, whizzed in a blender with ½ cup water

2 teaspoons grated fresh ginger

2 green chillies, finely chopped

1 teaspoon salt

1 teaspoon turmeric powder

3 teaspoons garam masala

2 handfuls of chopped coriander

½ cup black-eyed peas, soaked overnight and drained (but do not discard the water)

3 potatoes, peeled and cut into smallish cubes

Coconut rose barfi with sugared rose petals

The actual origins of St Valentine's Day and the myths surrounding the Saint himself are shrouded in Christian legend. For most people, this February occasion has come to represent a day of sheer commercialism, with a thin filmy coating of romance. If you are racking your brains for a gift that is a little more personal and meaningful than flowers, teddy bears and chocolate, why not go to the effort of making these coconut and rose Indian fudge truffles, complete with a topping of sugared, crystallised real rose petals. They are very easy to make and, when presented in a beautiful gift box, will surely find their way into anyone's heart. *Makes 25*

Method

1 Place the milk powder and ¾ cup of water together in a saucepan and stir well on a very low heat until well combined. It will come together in a singular mass quite quickly and come away from the sides of the pan.

2 Dilute the sugar in the remaining ¼ cup of water with the rose water. Add this, half of the coconut and the cochineal food colouring to the pan and stir very well. Keep stirring on a low heat until the mixture becomes thick – about 5 minutes after it has begun to come away from the sides of the pan.

3 Turn into a non-stick baking tray and spread evenly with a palette knife.

4 Sprinkle with the remaining coconut and refrigerate for 6 hours.

5 In the meantime, carefully remove the petals from the rose heads. Brush each petal lightly with egg white and then, holding it with your left fingertips over a bowl of caster sugar, use a teaspoon to cascade sugar over each side of the petal. Shake off any excess and set on a piece of greaseproof paper. Leave aside for a couple of hours.

6 Using your fingers, divide the chilled *barfi* mixture into 25 equal portions and roll into little balls.

7 Place on a platter topped with the rose petals and chill for a further hour at least before serving.

225 g (8 oz) milk powder

1 cup water

50 g (2 oz) caster sugar

5 tablespoons rose water

50 g (2 oz) fine desiccated coconut

few drops artificial cochineal food colouring

3 pink rose heads

1 egg white

½ cup caster sugar

Banana and green sultana raita

You've just weighed yourself after failing to zip up your favourite pair of jeans and realise you've put on a stone from Christmas excess. In your Bridget Jones mode you've thrown out all fattening substances, given up all your vices and have just bought an extortionately expensive membership at the gym. Before caving in on your first day of dieting, after only eating a head of lettuce all day, relieve your sugar cravings with this very healthy, natural yogurt dessert made from banana, Indian green sultanas (although if you can't find this variety use golden unsweetened sultanas instead), coconut and a smidgen of honey – organic if possible. Food that's good for you can taste wonderful too. Just don't eat it with a side portion of cake. *Serves 4–6*

Method

6 bananas, diced

500 g carton natural bio yogurt

¼ cup green sultanas

2 tablespoons desiccated coconut

drizzle of honey

1 Place the bananas, yogurt and sultanas in a dish and stir to mix.

2 Sprinkle with coconut and drizzle with honey.

Fennel tea *Saunf wali chaa*

When I first heard of Fairtrade a few years ago, there was no turning back. And today there is more choice than ever with a range of products that are of extremely high quality.

I started with the tea bags. Coming from a typical British-Asian family, I personally know how much British Asians love their sweet, hot, milky tea – or *chaa* as we call it. As a teenager, I seemed to be forever making vatfuls for roomfuls of relatives and *auntyjis*. If every British-Asian family switched to using Fairtrade tea bags, that would be a huge victory in itself!

And it doesn't stop there. There are so many opportunities to use Fairtrade products within the British-Asian kitchen. Along with the recipe in this book for Cardamom and Gold Chocolate Truffles (page 56) and the recipe here for Fennel Tea, you can also buy Fairtrade sweet mangoes to eat after *roti*, lemons to make *achaar*, and biscuits to offer to guests, to mention just a few.

But how do these products taste you might ask? Let me assure you, every Fairtrade product I have tried, and believe me I have munched my way through a lot, was extremely tasty and in some cases, such as Fairtrade chocolate, better than any non-Fairtrade product I have tasted. But no food tastes as sweet as that eaten with a clear conscience. *Serves 4*

Method

1 Place the water in a pan with the brown and green cardamoms, fennel seeds and green sultanas or raisins. Bring to the boil. Boil for 5 minutes.

2 Add the tea bag and continue to boil for about 3 minutes.

3 Add enough milk so that it looks a little too pale. Bring to the boil again and, just as it reaches the top of the pan, turn the heat down very low. Simmer for another couple of minutes.

4 Strain and pour into cups or glasses. Add sugar to taste.

5 cups water

1 brown cardamom, lightly bashed in a pestle and mortar

2 green cardamoms, lightly bashed in a pestle and mortar

1 tablespoon fennel seeds

1 tablespoon green sultanas or raisins

1 Fairtrade tea bag

milk

Glossary of terms

Various Punjabi, Hindi, Urdu and Gujarati words are used throughout the book; if any are unfamiliar, look them up here.

achaar	~	pickle
adrak	~	fresh root ginger
ajwain	~	carom seeds
aloo tikkia	~	fried potato patties
aloo	~	potato
amchoor	~	dried mango powder
anardhana	~	pomegranate seed powder
atta	~	wheat flour
auntyji	~	term of respect for an older, unrelated female
ayurvedic	~	the holistic life science developed in India in which a diet balanced in accordance with a person's constitution plays a very important role
badaam	~	almonds
balti	~	as popularised in Birmingham, another name for a *karahi* – the metal dish used to stir-fry certain meat dishes
bandhan	~	to tie
barfi	~	an Indian sweet made from milk
barri elaichi	~	large brown cardamoms
belan	~	rolling pin
besan	~	*gram* flour/chickpea flour
bhangra	~	Punjabi folk music, now set to modern beats and very popular in British-Asian youth culture
bhati	~	frying pan
bhoondi	~	deep-fried *gram* flour balls
Bibiji	~	our family term for my grandmother
bindia	~	the little adhesive, colourful, decorative and often jewelled adornments worn on the foreheads of Indian females on special occasions
biryani	~	baked rice dish
chaat	~	popular South Indian street snack
chachiji	~	aunt (Dad's younger brother's wife)
chakla	~	small round wooden chopping board
chamche	~	spoons

chana dhal	~	split chickpeas
chaul	~	rice
chimta	~	tongs
chole	~	chickpeas, also known as *channe*
chunnia	~	chiffon scarves, worn either draped over the shoulders or over the head by Indian women
dahi	~	natural yogurt
dalchini	~	cassia bark or cinnamon
Deepavali	~	the full Sanskrit name for the festival of Diwali
dhaak	~	sultanas
dhala	~	pulses
dhaniya daana	~	coriander seeds
dhaniya	~	coriander leaves
dhokla	~	*gram* flour sponge
dive/diye	~	little lamps or lights
Diwali	~	Hindu and Sikh festival of lights
dosa	~	South Indian pancake
elaichi	~	green cardamoms
falooda	~	dessert that is a cross between a milkshake and a sundae
gajar	~	carrot
gandha	~	onion, also known as *piaj* or *piaz*
garam masala	~	indispensable blend of powdered spices
garba	~	Gujarati festival dance, sometimes with sticks
giddha	~	Punjabi folk dance
golgappe	~	also known as *pani puri*, these are deep-fried, hollow crispy spheres with a very thin shell
gram flour	~	chickpea flour also known as *besan*
gur	~	jaggery, a solid sugar made from sugar cane
Gurudwara	~	Sikh temple
haldi	~	turmeric powder
hanji	~	respectful way of answering 'yes' to your elders in Punjabi
hari mirch	~	fresh green chillies
hing	~	also known as *asafoetida*
idli	~	South Indian steamed rice cakes
imli	~	tamarind
jalebia	~	syrupy, crispy, orange batter coils

jihad	~	literally means religious struggle – can be taken to mean struggle with oneself to be a better person, or can also mean a holy war
kala jeera	~	black cumin seeds
kali mirch	~	black pepper
kalonji	~	nigella seeds
karah prasad	~	sweet distributed as a grace at the *Gurudwara*
karahi	~	the metal dish used to stir-fry certain meat dishes, commonly used in North India
karchhi	~	traditional large metal spoon
kasoori methi	~	dried fenugreek
keema	~	minced meat
kesar	~	saffron
kewra	~	screwpine essence used to flavour Indian desserts
khichidi	~	rice and lentil dish
kirtan	~	Sikh hymns sung in the *gurudwara*
kofte	~	usually meatballs, but can be vegetarian, too
laal mirch	~	red chillies
lahsun	~	garlic
lassi	~	yogurt drink
laung	~	cloves
luhn	~	salt
makhan	~	butter
mattar	~	peas
mendhi	~	henna, often worn in elaborate patterns on the palms of Indian women during weddings
methi daana	~	fenugreek seeds
methi	~	fenugreek leaves
mittai	~	generic term for Indian sweets
mogo	~	deep-fried cassava chips, served with lemon juice; a Gujarati speciality
moong dhal	~	whole mung beans
Mummyji	~	Mum
naan	~	leavened bread cooked in a *tandoor*
nimbu	~	lemon or lime
panch puran	~	blend of five pickling spices
paneer	~	firm, mild Indian cream cheese

pani pooria	~	another term for *golgappe*
Papiji	~	our family term for our grandfather
paratha/parathe	~	fried bread(s)
pathila	~	saucepan
phaal	~	ultra-hot British curry house dish, similar to a *vindaloo*
phirni	~	rice-based dessert
phupherji	~	uncle (husband of aunt on Dad's side of the family)
pista	~	pistachio nuts
pooiji	~	aunt on Dad's side of the family
poori(a)/puri(s)	~	deep-fried crispy bread(s)
raara	~	the stage in cooking a *tarka* when the oil separates from the spices
rai daana	~	black mustard seeds
raita	~	yogurt accompaniment made with vegetables and spices
Rakhria	~	the Punjabi popular term for the festival of Raksha Bandhan
raksha	~	to protect
rangoli	~	popular Indian art using coloured powders
rongi dhal	~	dried red kidney beans
rooh afza	~	rose syrup
roti	~	not only the term for the Indian bread more commonly known as a *chapati*, it is also a generic term for an Indian meal
sabji/sabjia	~	although this term refers to vegetable (and occasionally some fish) dishes, which have been cooked in the appropriate way, it also means raw vegetables
samosa/samose	~	deep-fried triangular filled pastry
saunf	~	fennel seeds
sev	~	crunchy noodles
sevian	~	vermicelli
sharbart	~	refreshing drink with ice or sorbet
suji	~	semolina
sukki laal mirch	~	dried red chilli flakes
tamatar	~	tomatoes
tandoor	~	clay oven used for cooking breads and some meat dishes
tandoori masala	~	spice blend used for *tandoori* dishes
tandoori	~	any food traditionally cooked in a *tandoor*
tarka	~	base for sauces
tej patta	~	bay leaves

tel	~	oil
thari	~	the name given to quite a runny sauce
thariwala	~	means 'with a runny sauce'
thawa	~	cast-iron griddle for cooking breads
thomi mahaar dhal	~	washed, split urid beans
tukmaria	~	seeds added to desserts – they swell upon being soaked and produce a cooling effect on the stomach; also known as *sabja* seeds
uncleji	~	term of respect for an older, unrelated male
urid	~	black lentil
zeera	~	cumin seeds

Acknowledgements

My most sincere thanks to my parents, my brother, Aneil, and sister, Karen; Simon and Schuster, particularly Kim Yarwood, Janet Copleston, Paula Borton, Kathy Gale, Jeremy Butcher, Sue Stephens, Caroline Turner; Jonny Ring; Kim Morphew; Juliet Piddington; Jane Humphrey; Kate Miller; Euan Thorneycroft at Curtis Brown.

Thank you for making this book happen and for all your hard work and support.